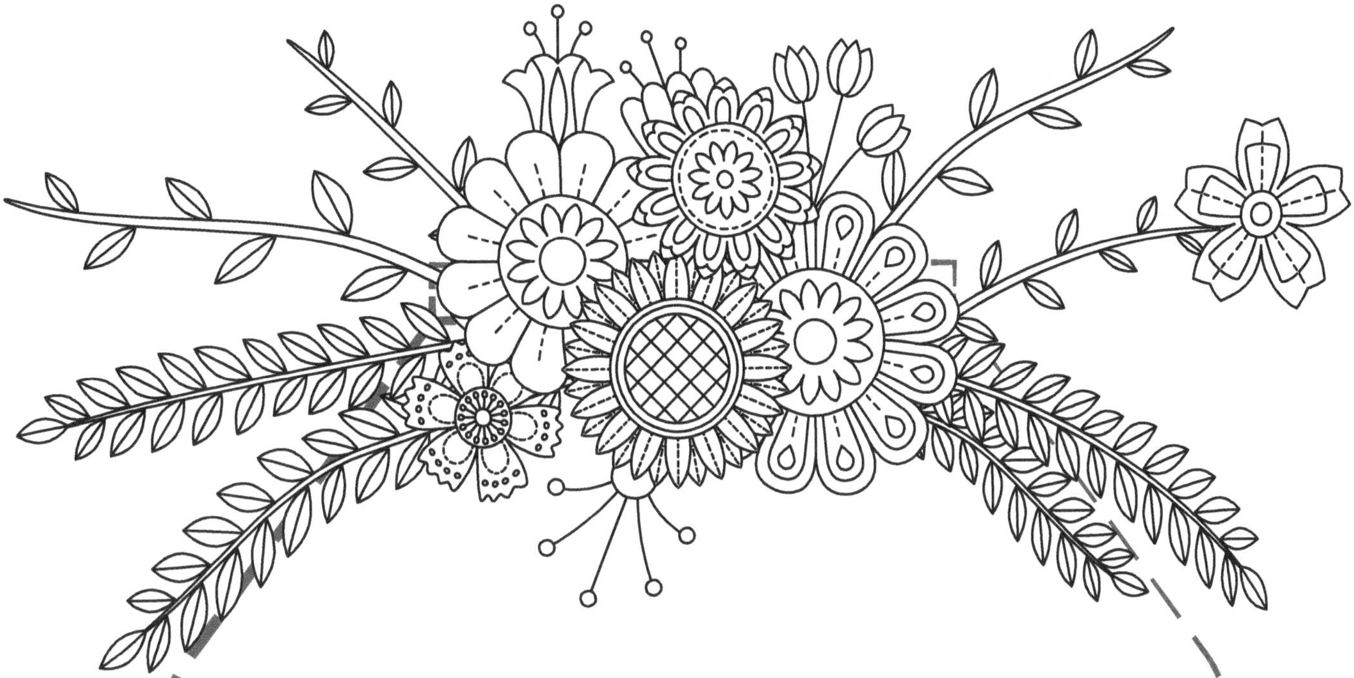

This Book Belongs To:

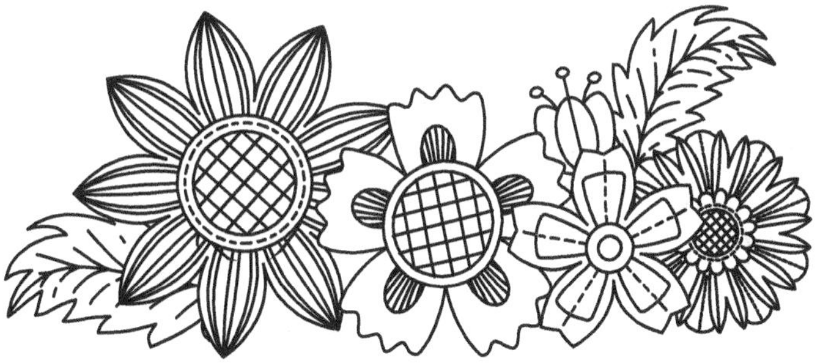

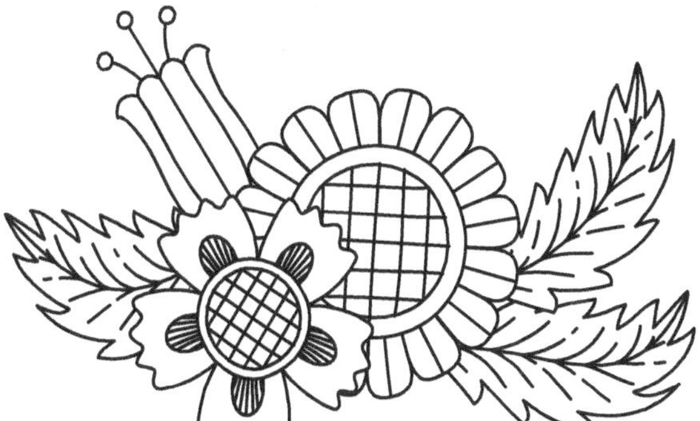

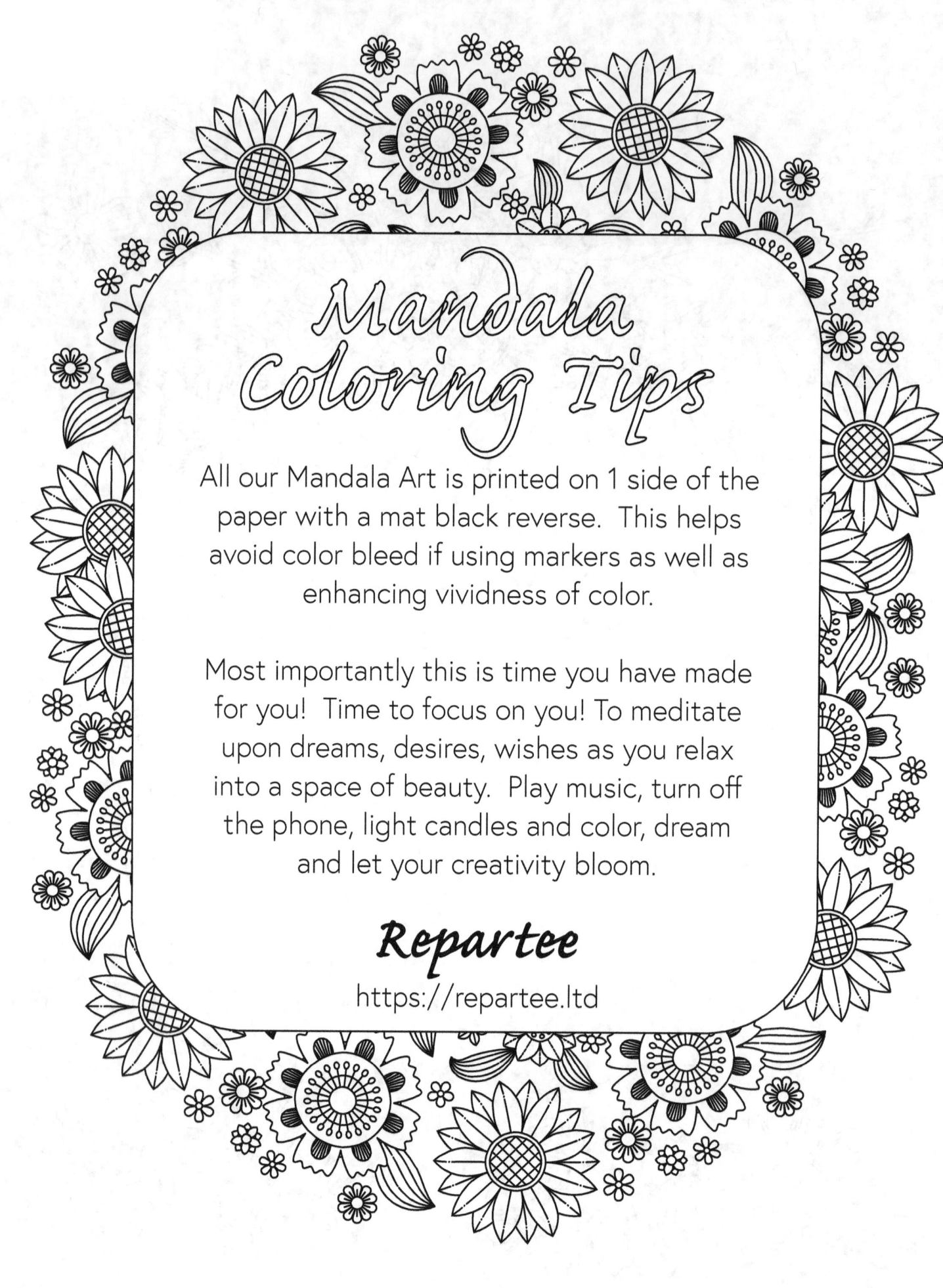

Mandala Coloring Tips

All our Mandala Art is printed on 1 side of the paper with a mat black reverse. This helps avoid color bleed if using markers as well as enhancing vividness of color.

Most importantly this is time you have made for you! Time to focus on you! To meditate upon dreams, desires, wishes as you relax into a space of beauty. Play music, turn off the phone, light candles and color, dream and let your creativity bloom.

Repartee

https://repartee.ltd

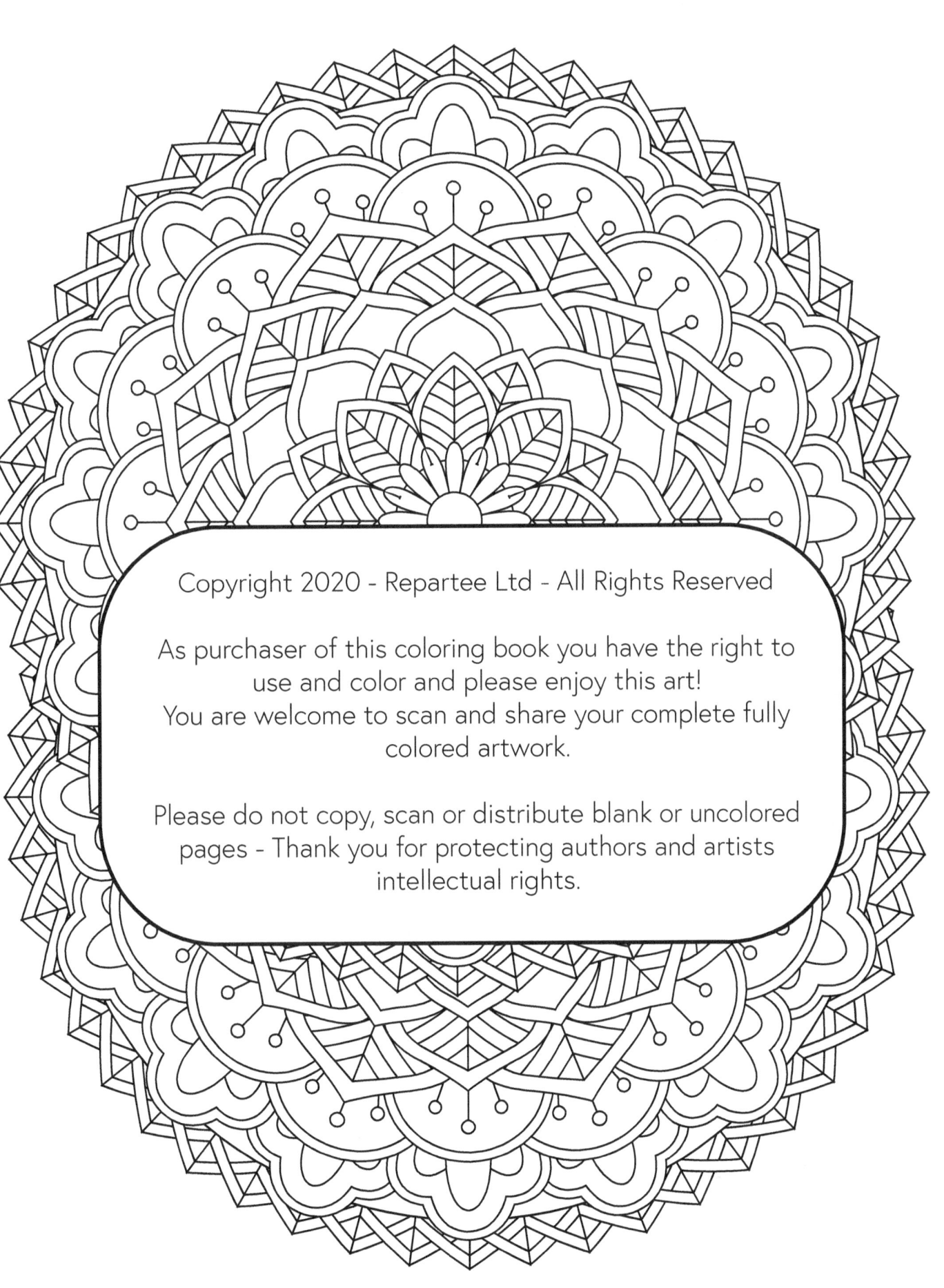

Copyright 2020 - Repartee Ltd - All Rights Reserved

As purchaser of this coloring book you have the right to use and color and please enjoy this art!
You are welcome to scan and share your complete fully colored artwork.

Please do not copy, scan or distribute blank or uncolored pages - Thank you for protecting authors and artists intellectual rights.

Reverse Mandala

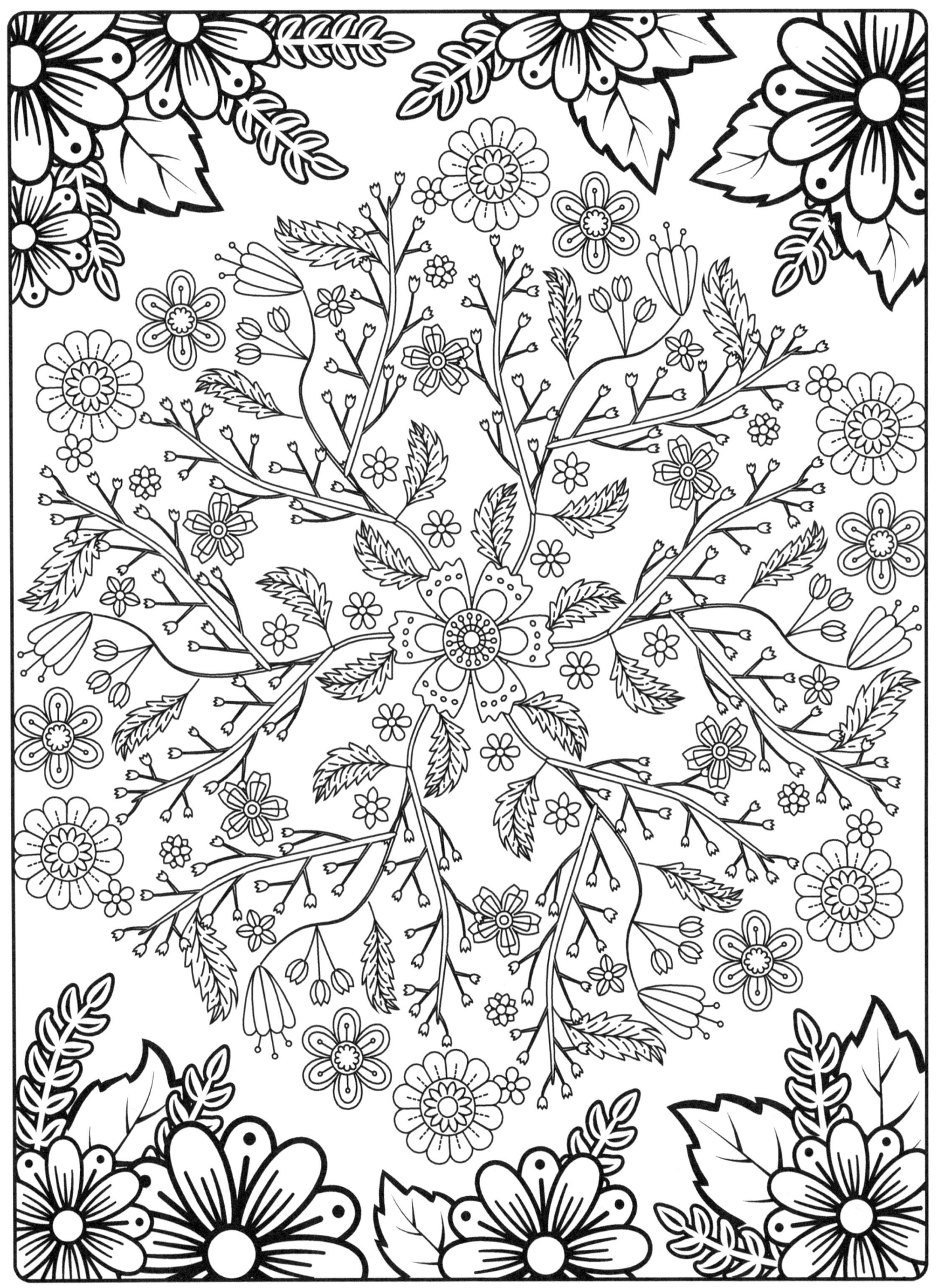

Reverse Mandala

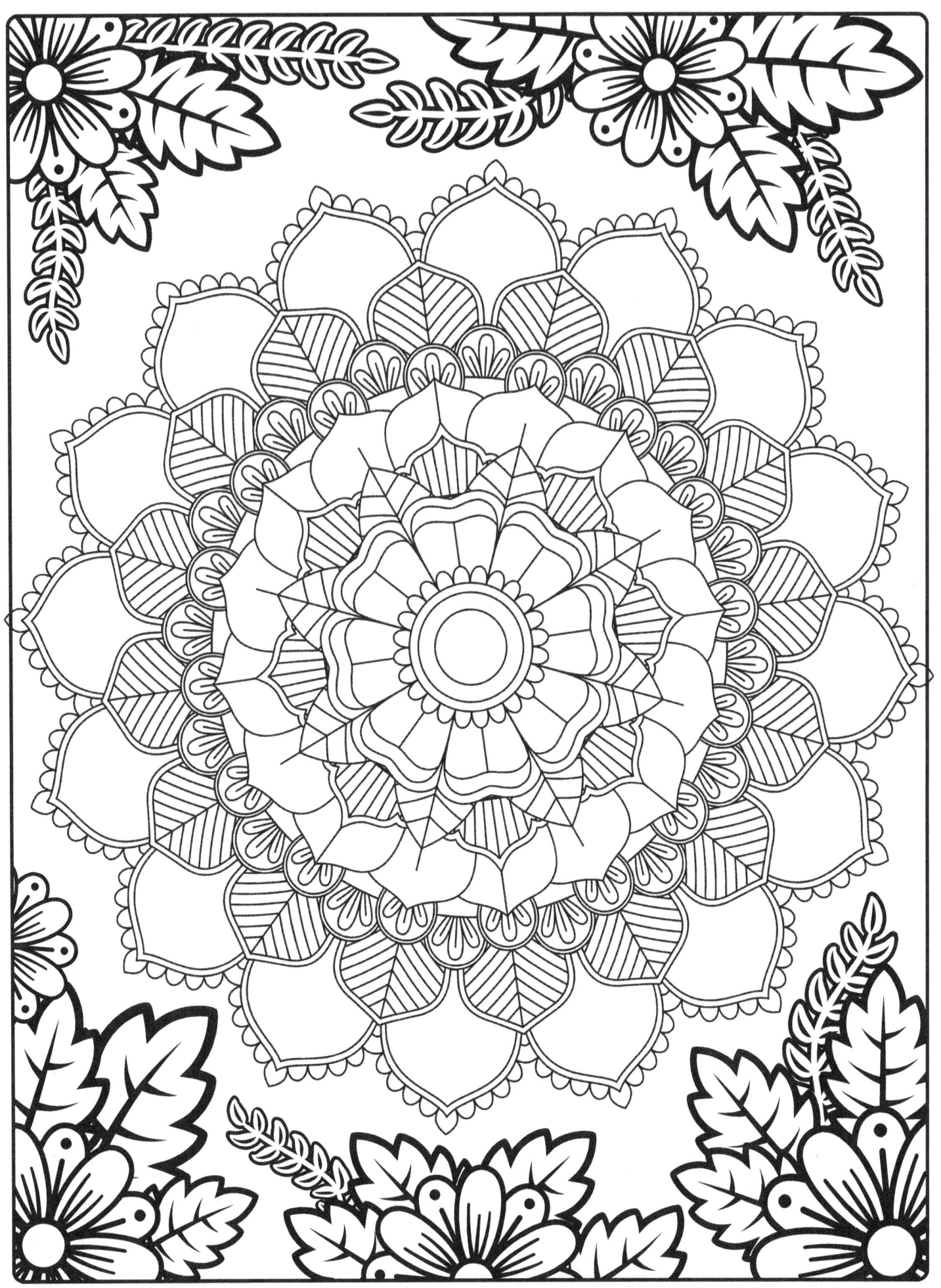

Reverse Mandala

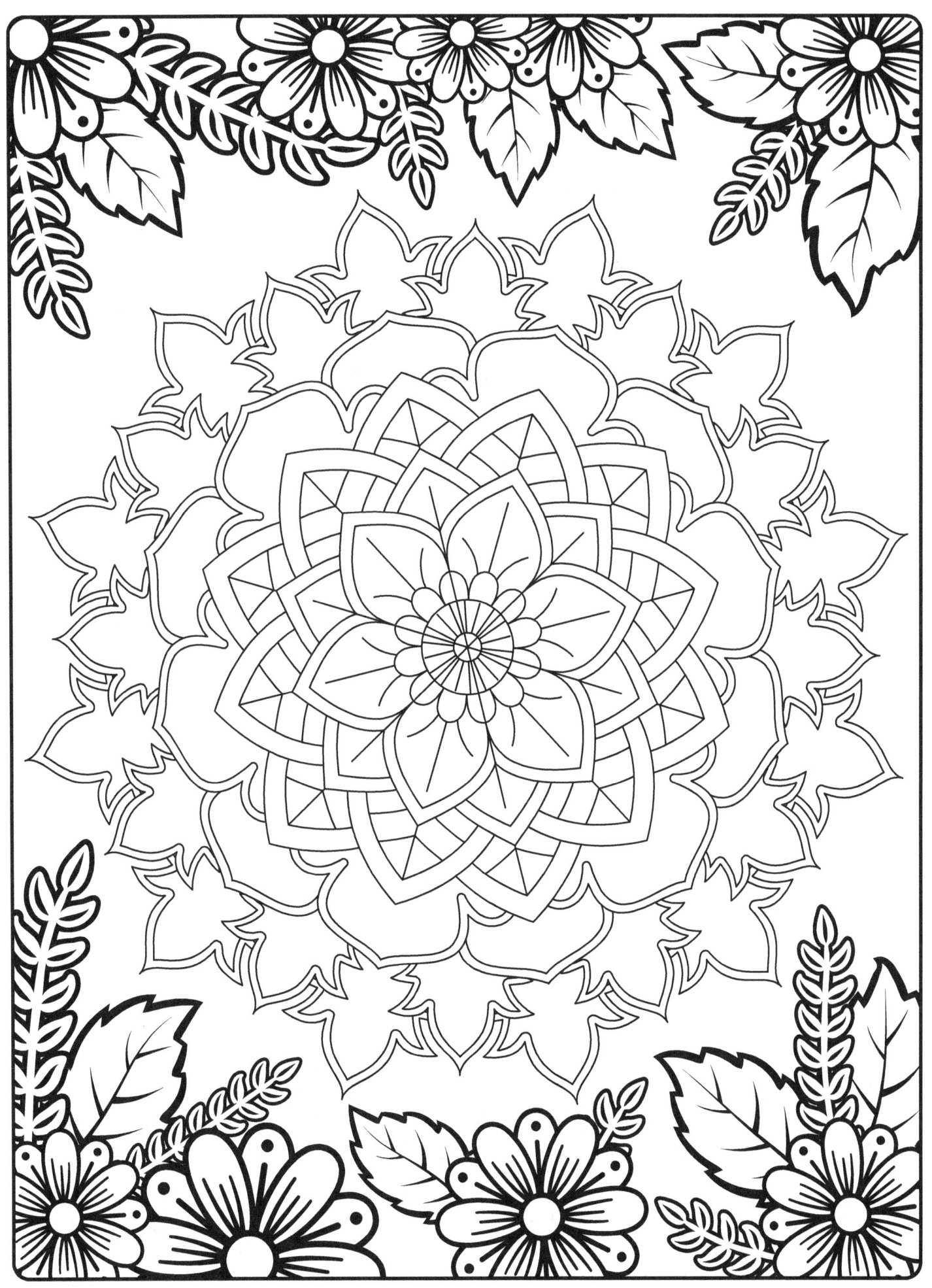

Reverse Mandala

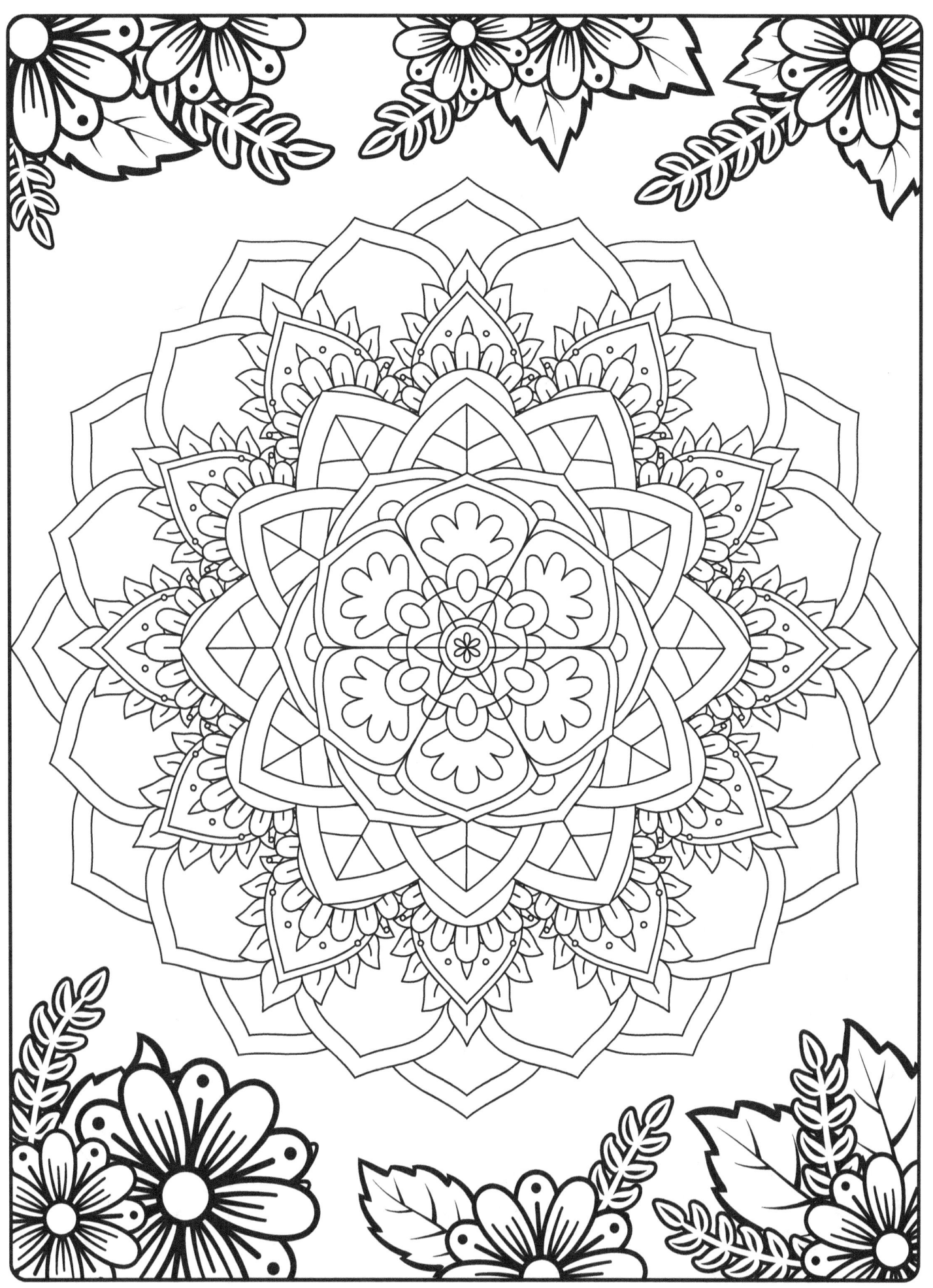

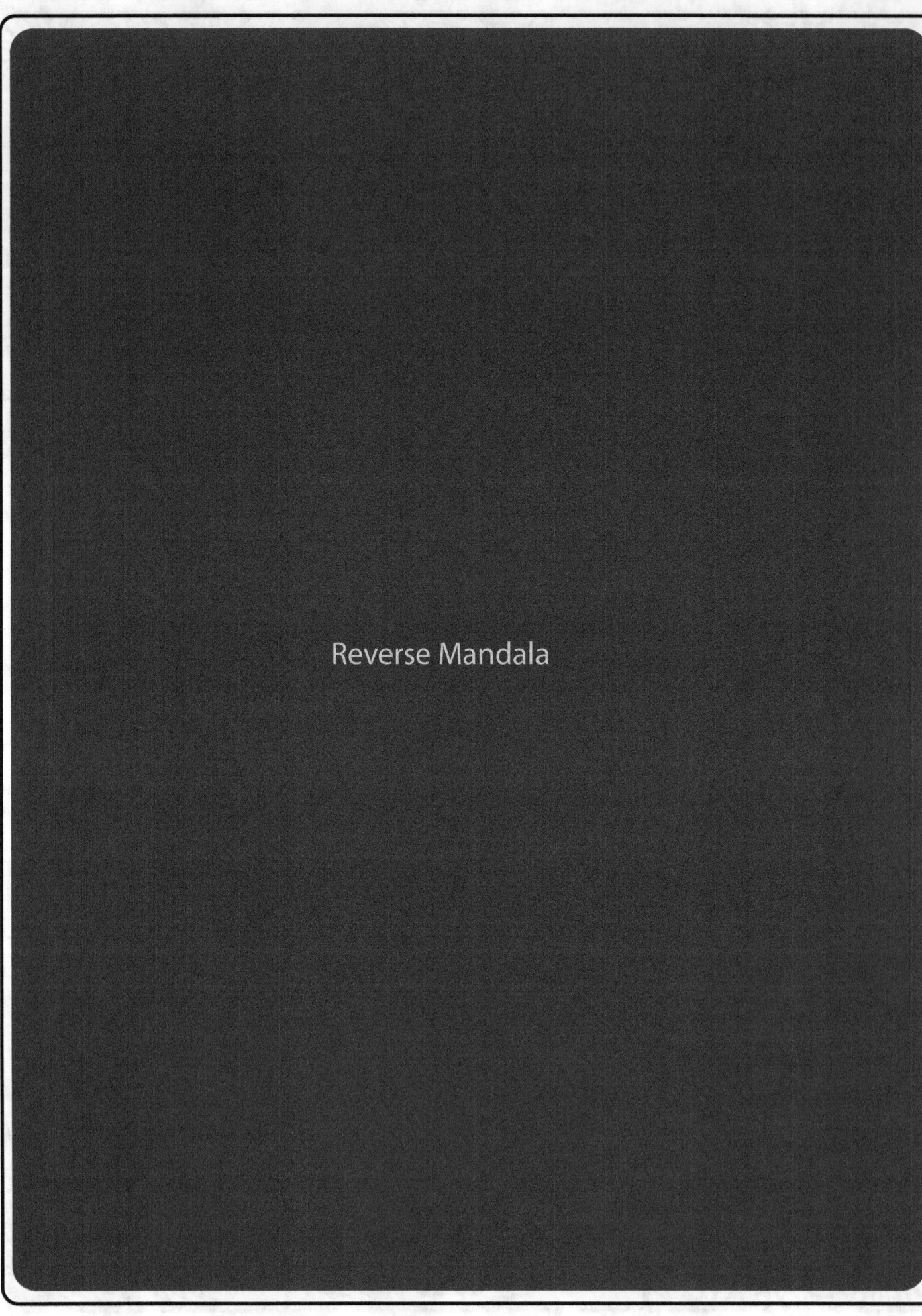

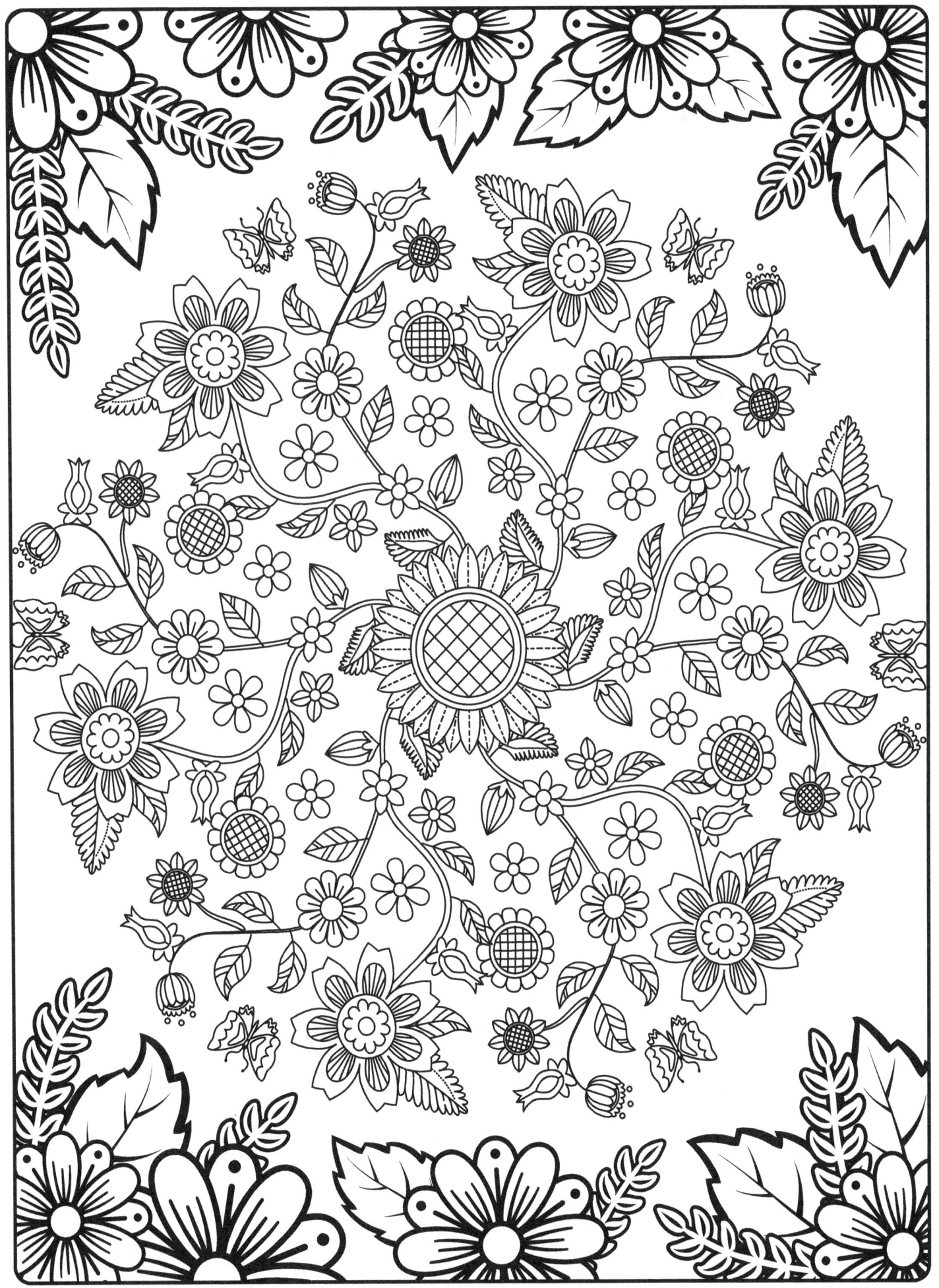

Reverse Mandala

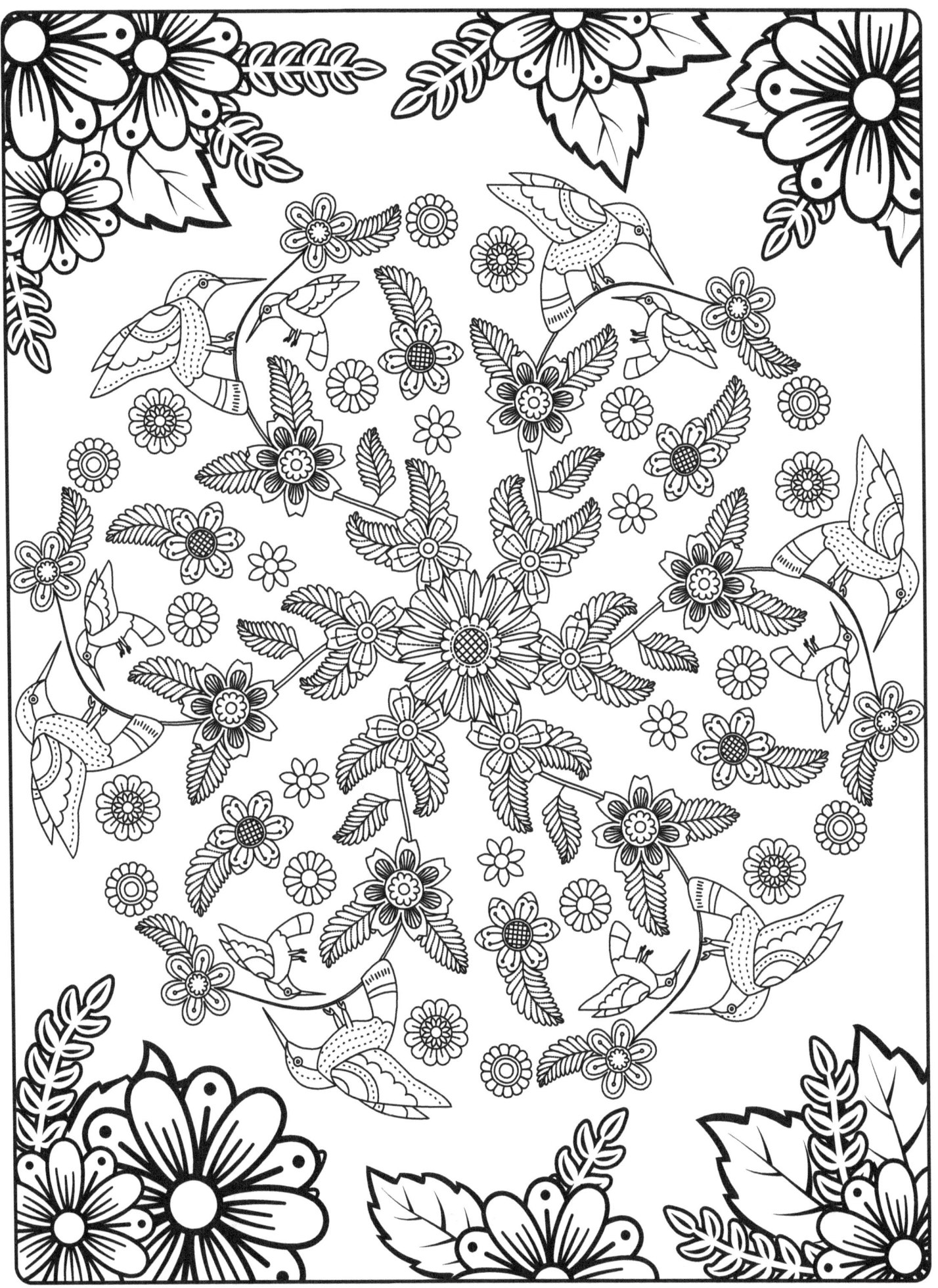

Reverse Mandala

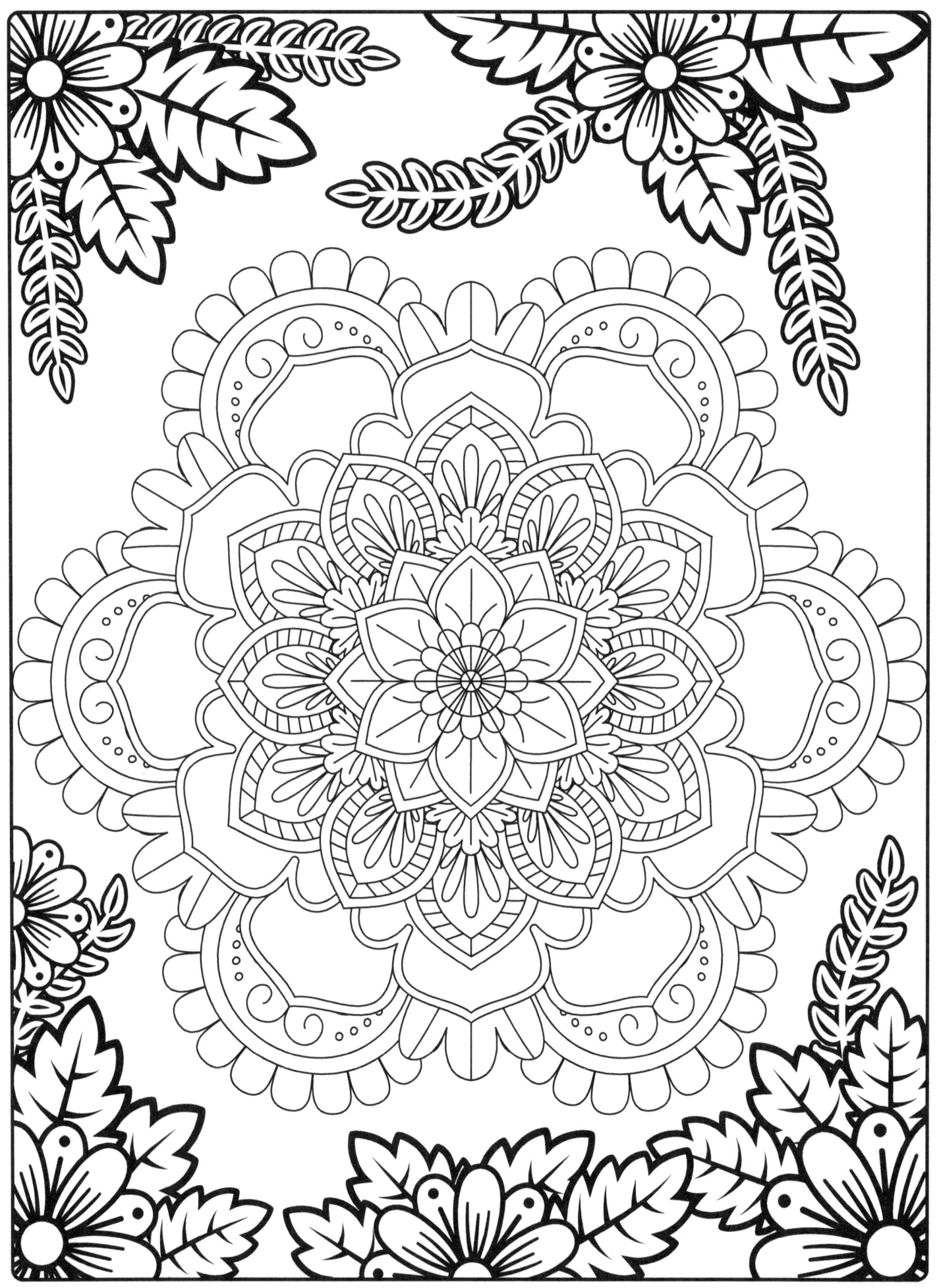

Reverse Mandala

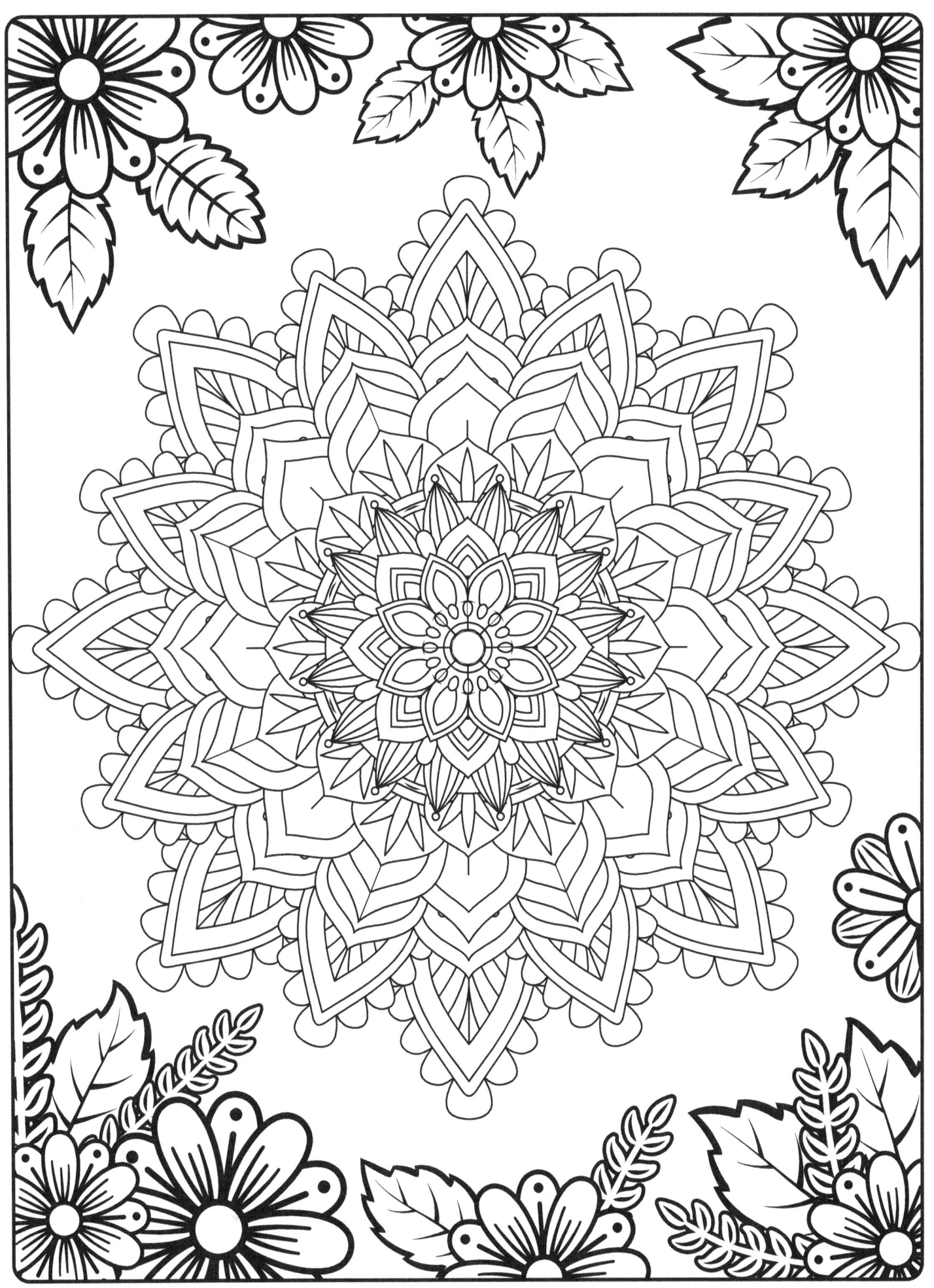

Reverse Mandala

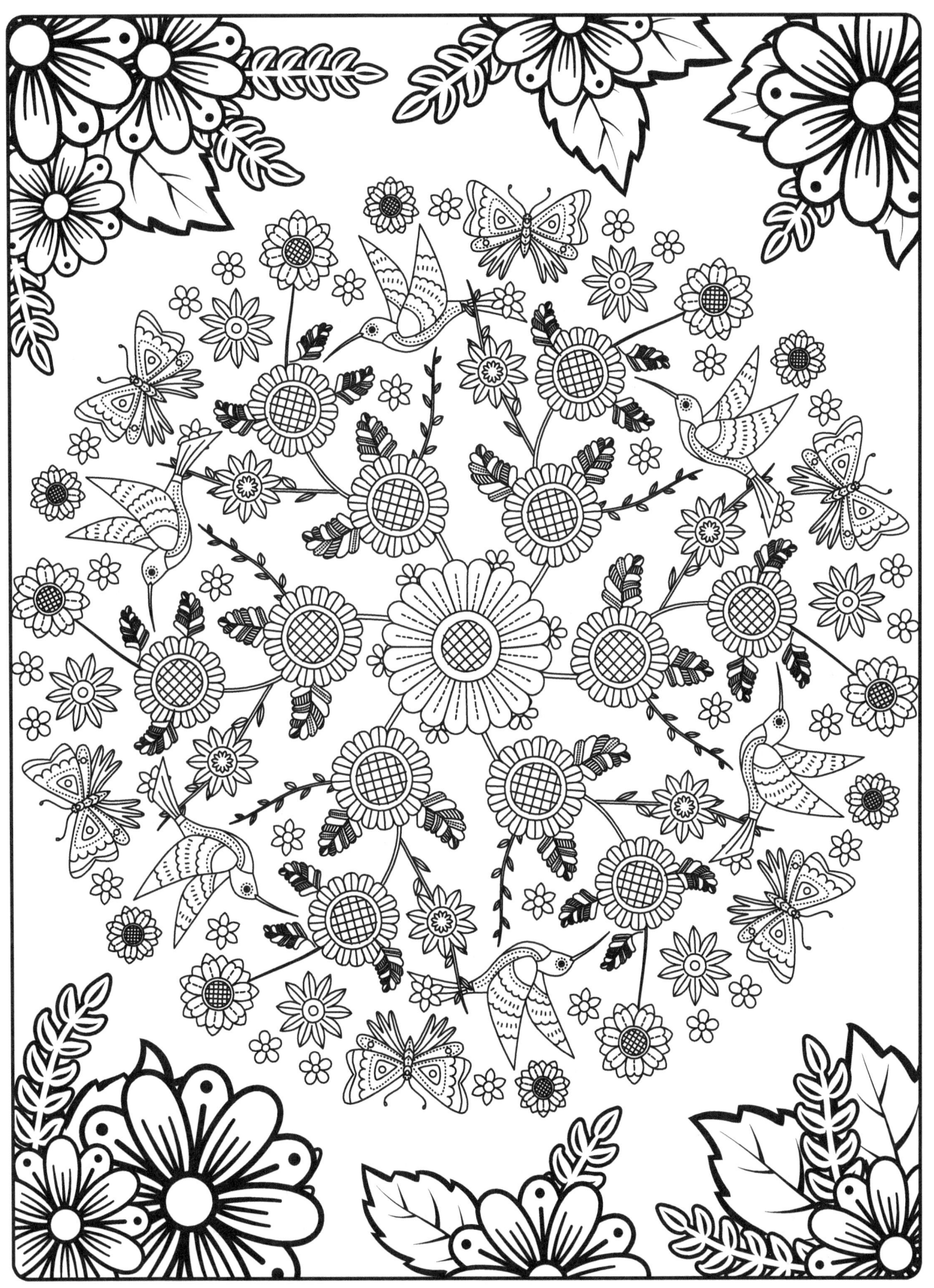

Reverse Mandala

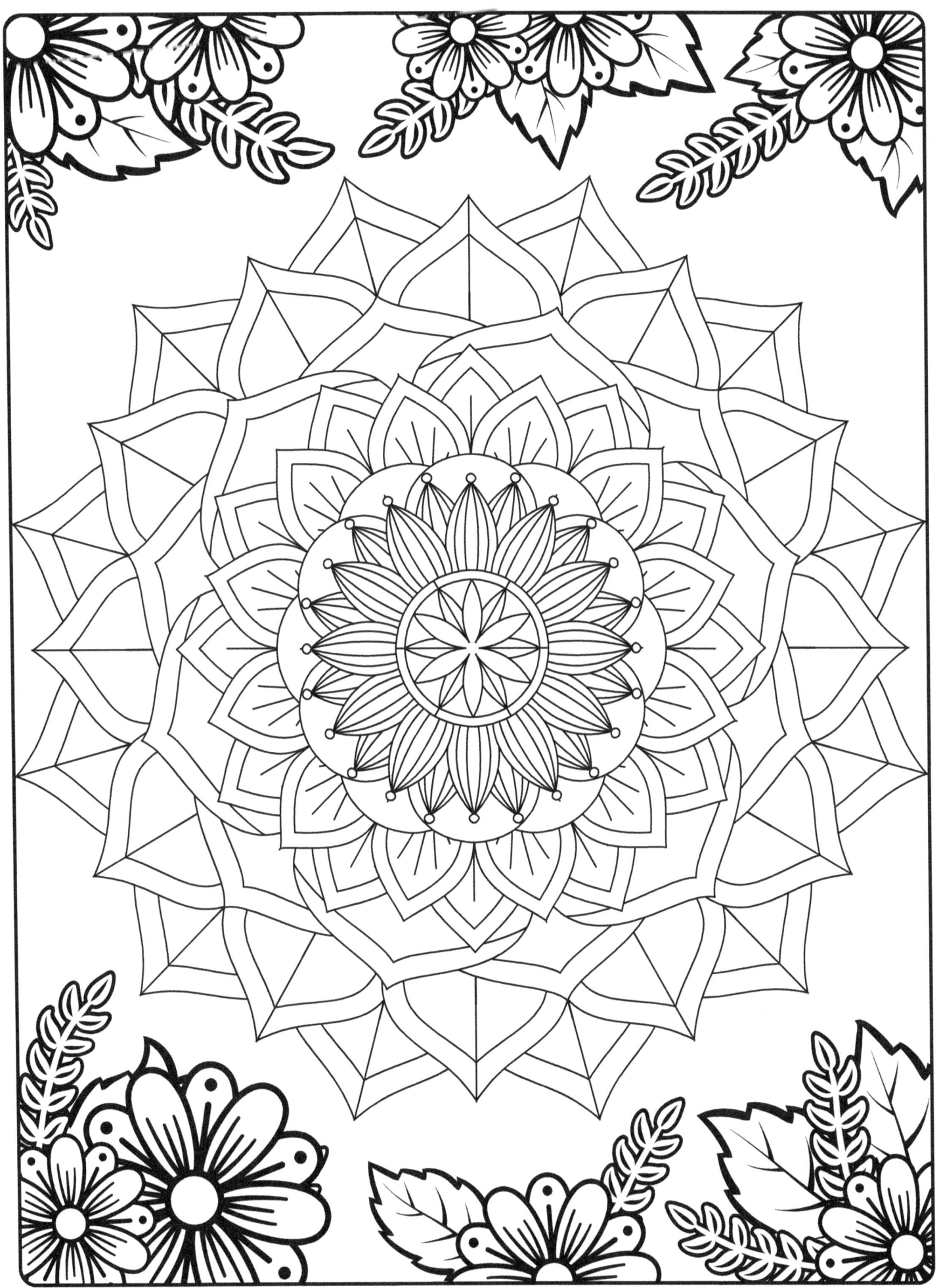

Reverse Mandala

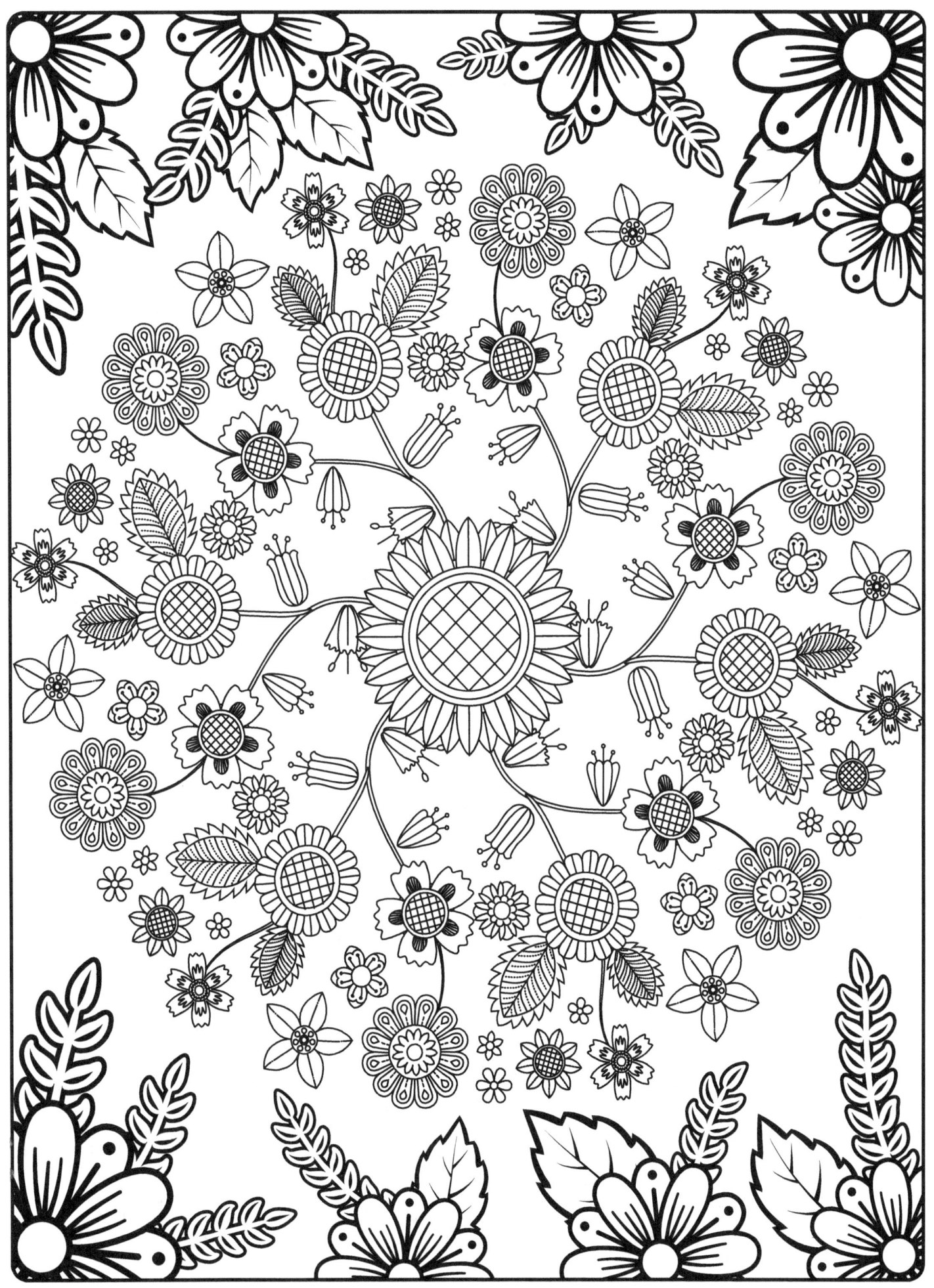

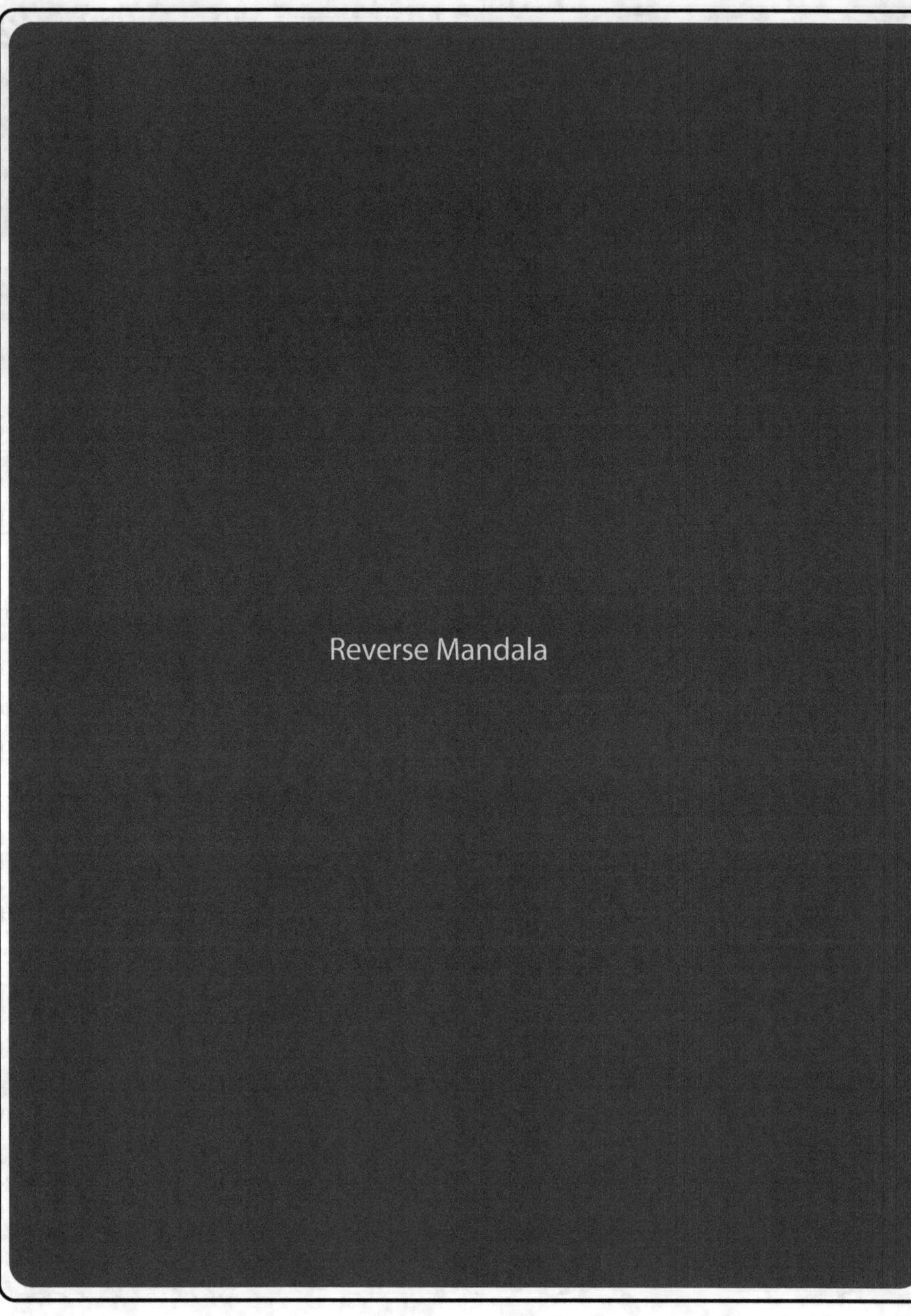

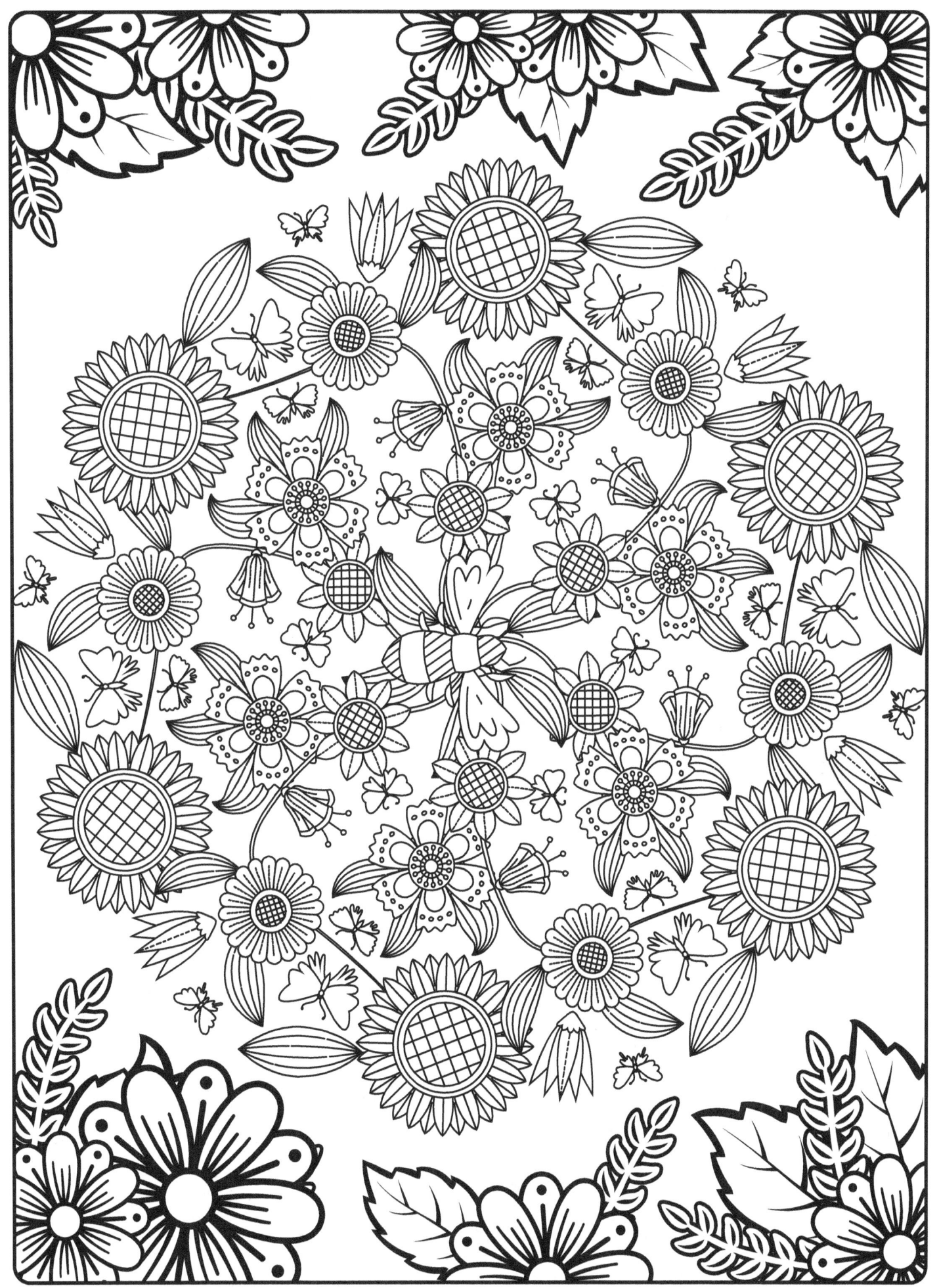

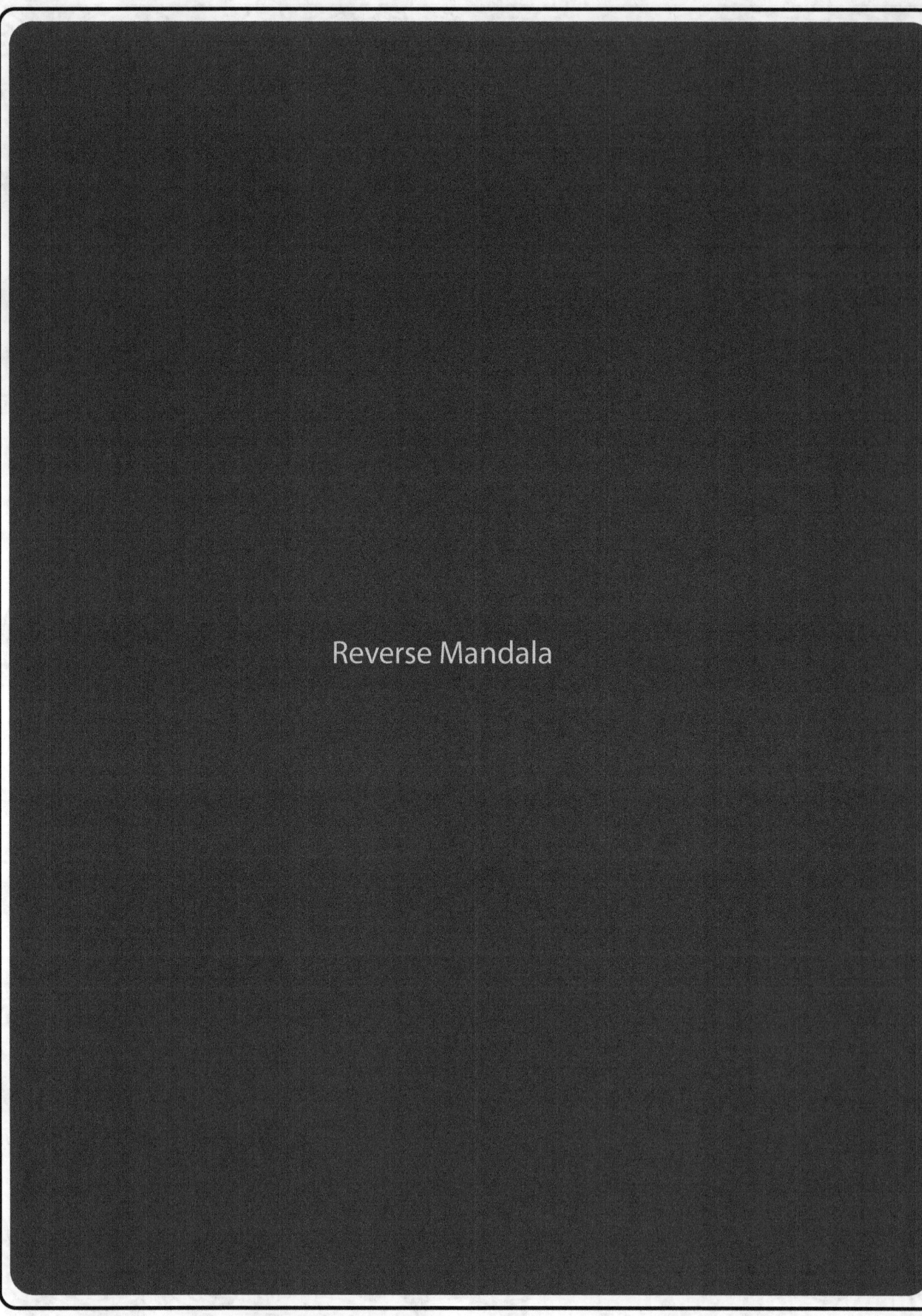

Reverse Mandala

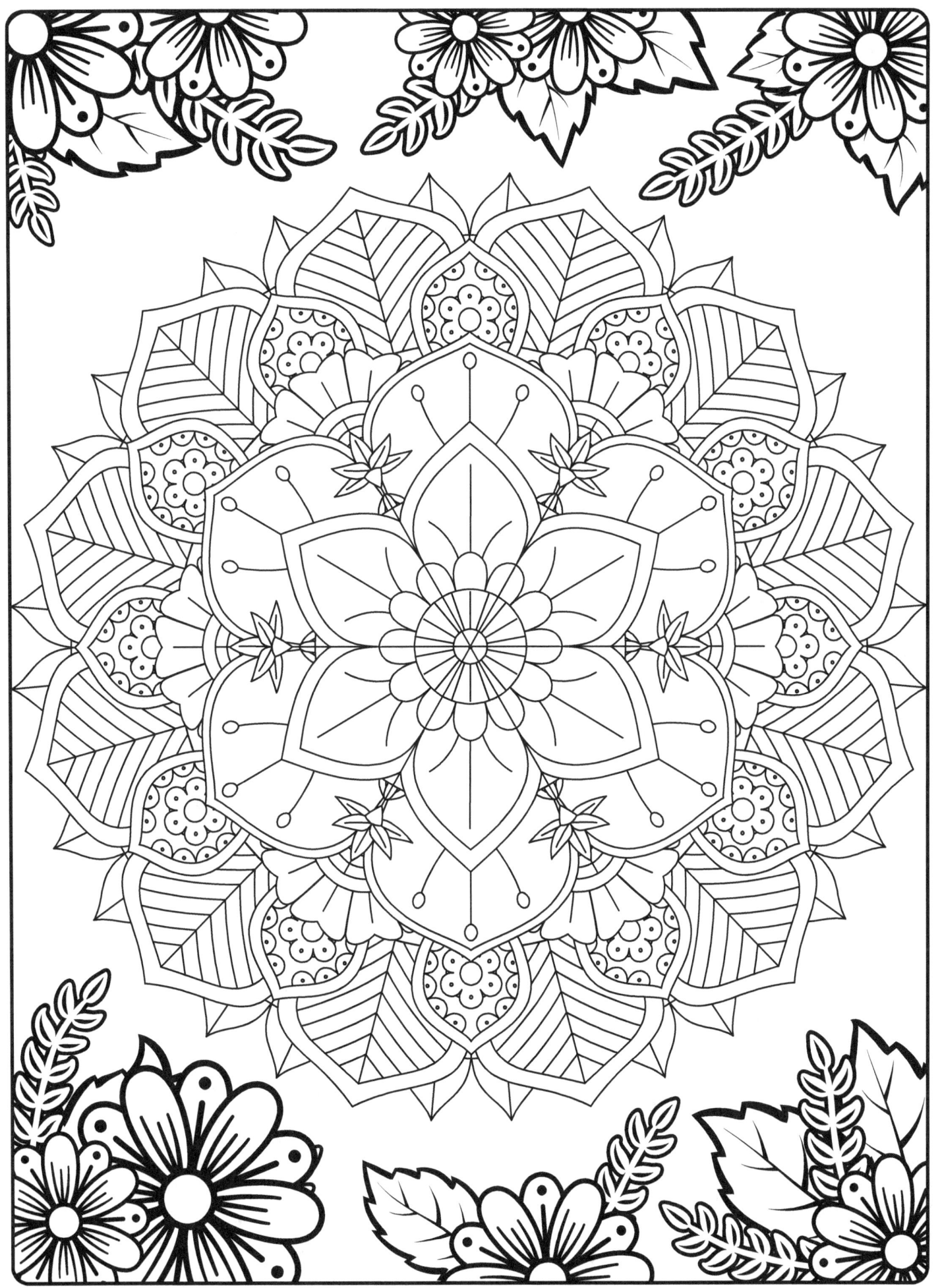

Reverse Mandala

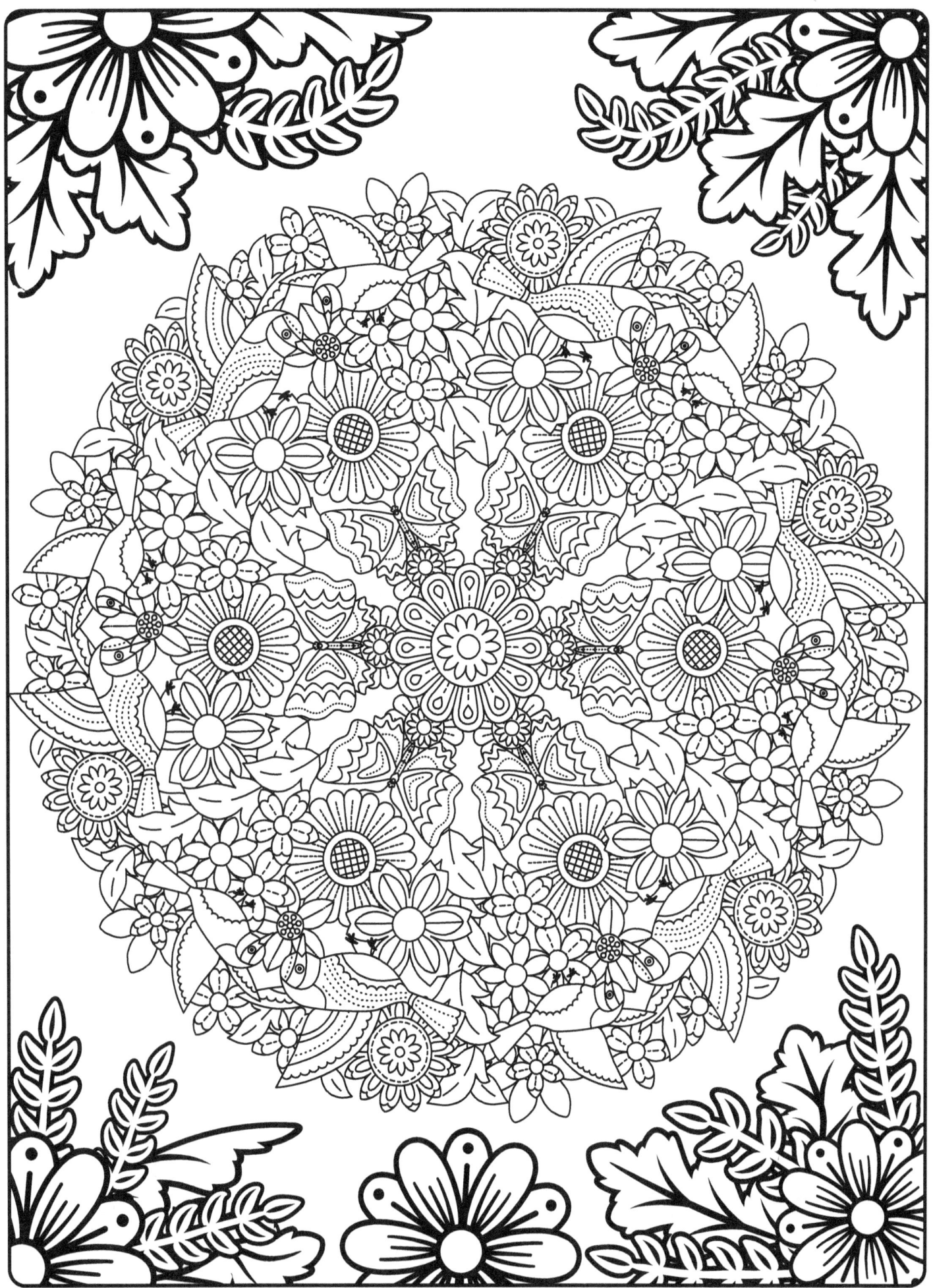

Reverse Mandala

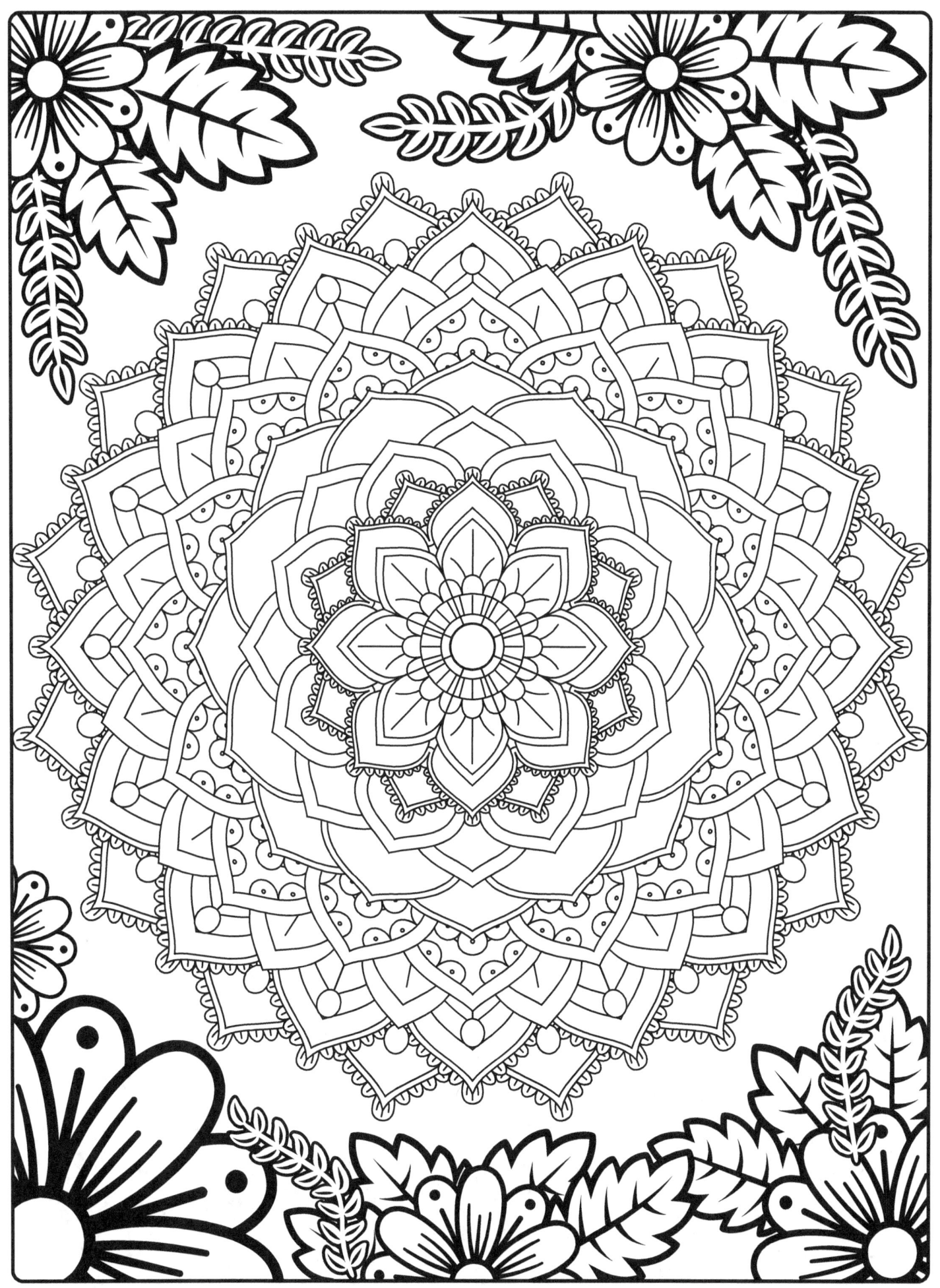

Reverse Mandala

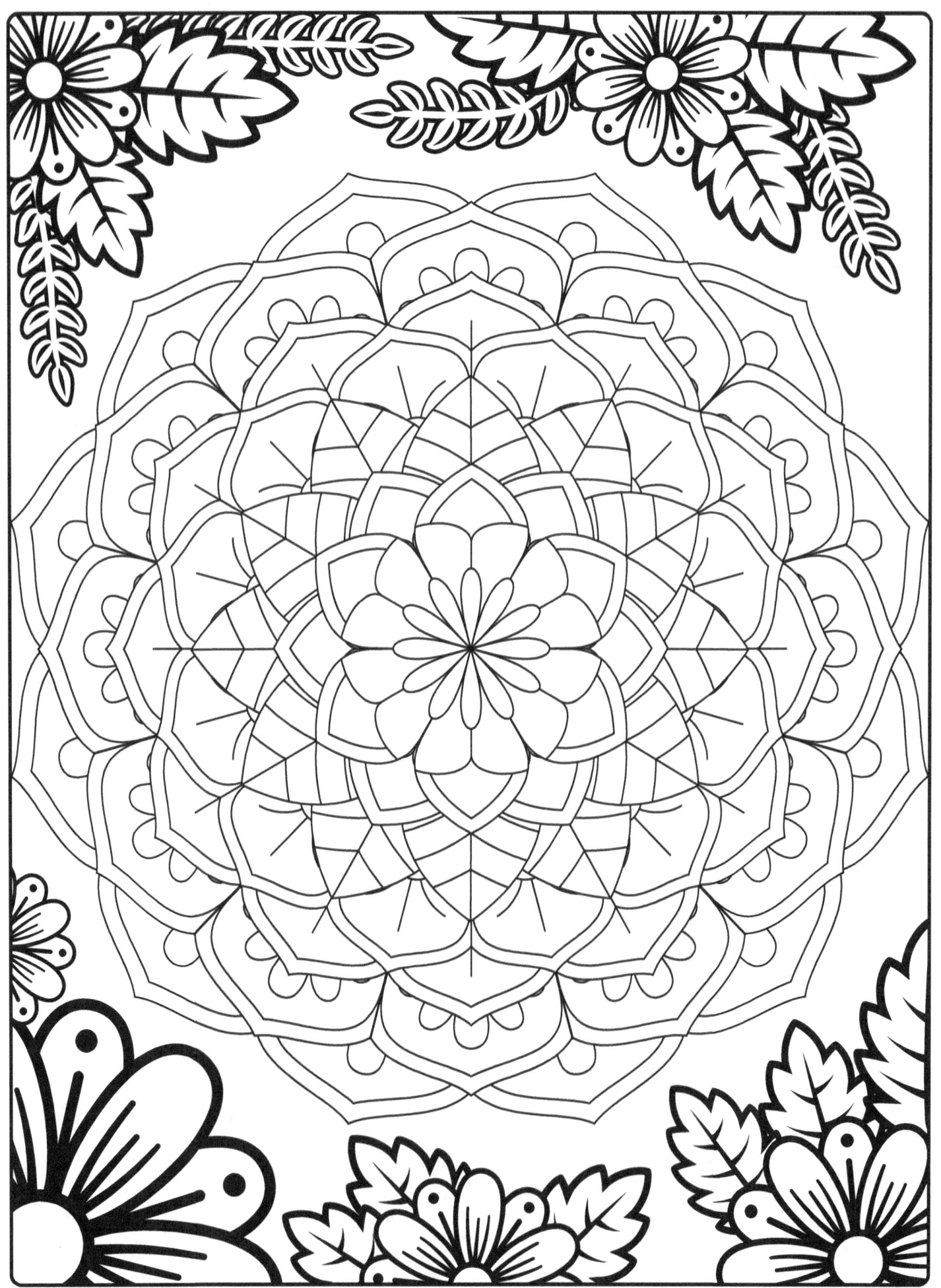

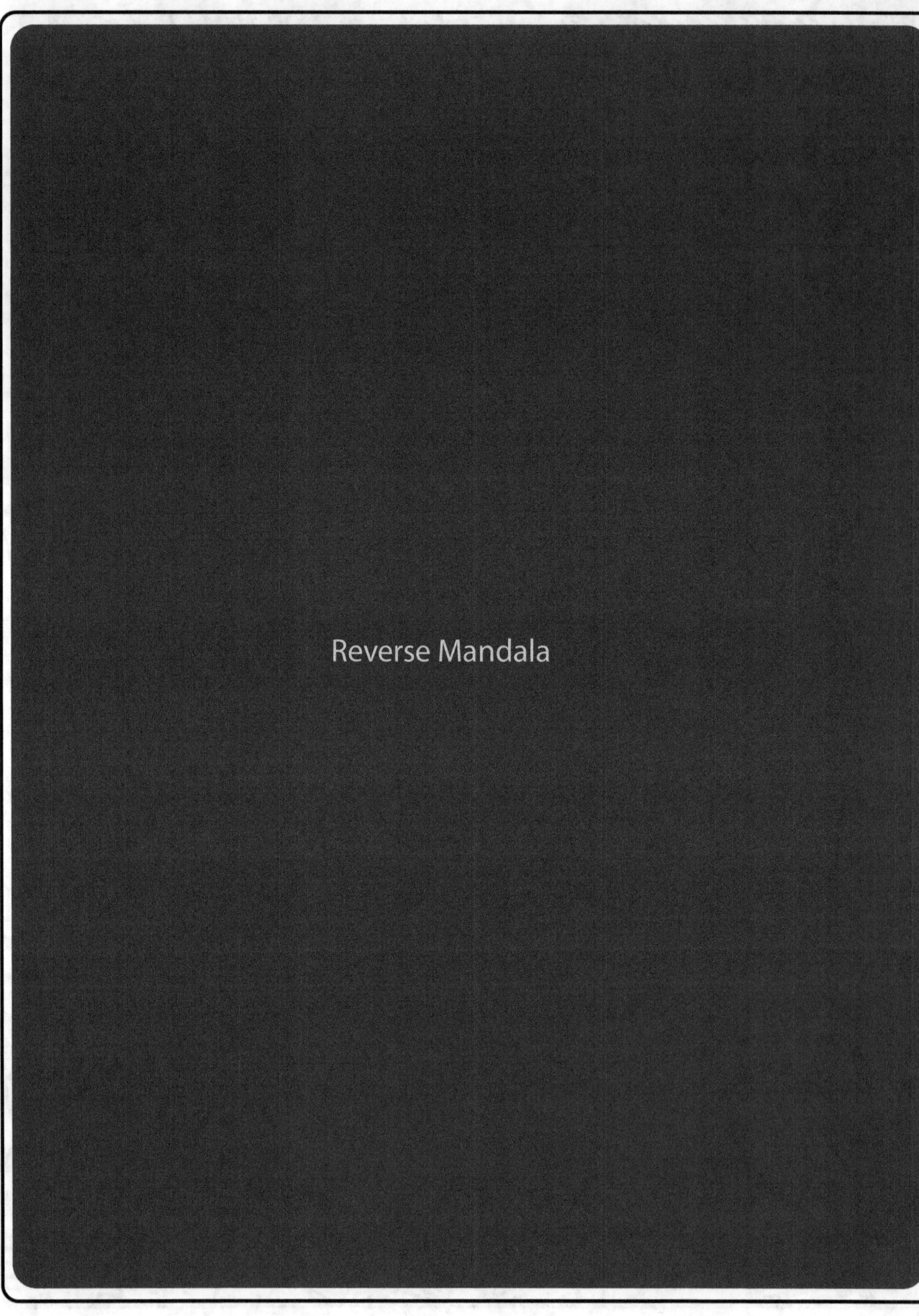

Reverse Mandala

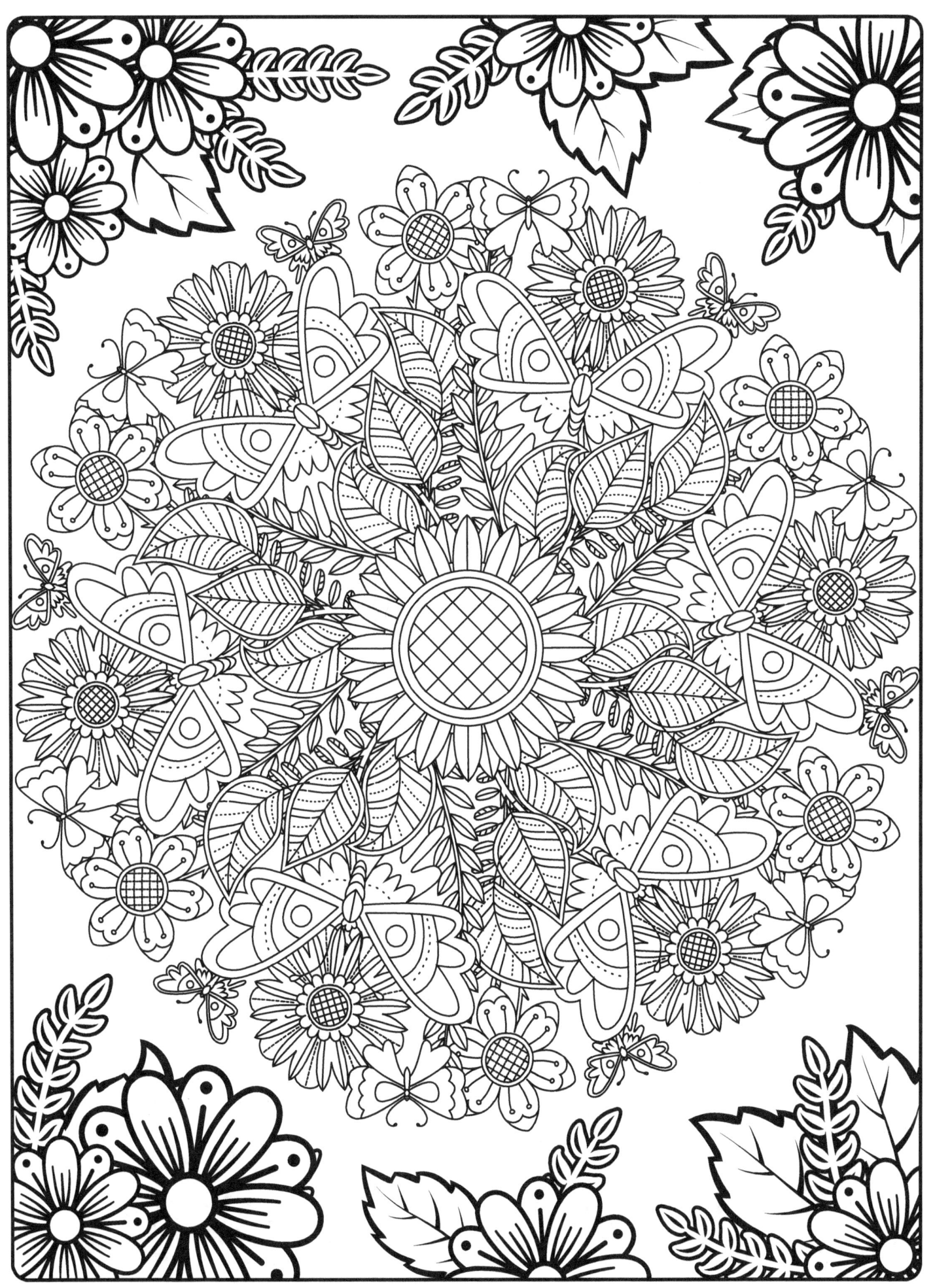

Reverse Mandala

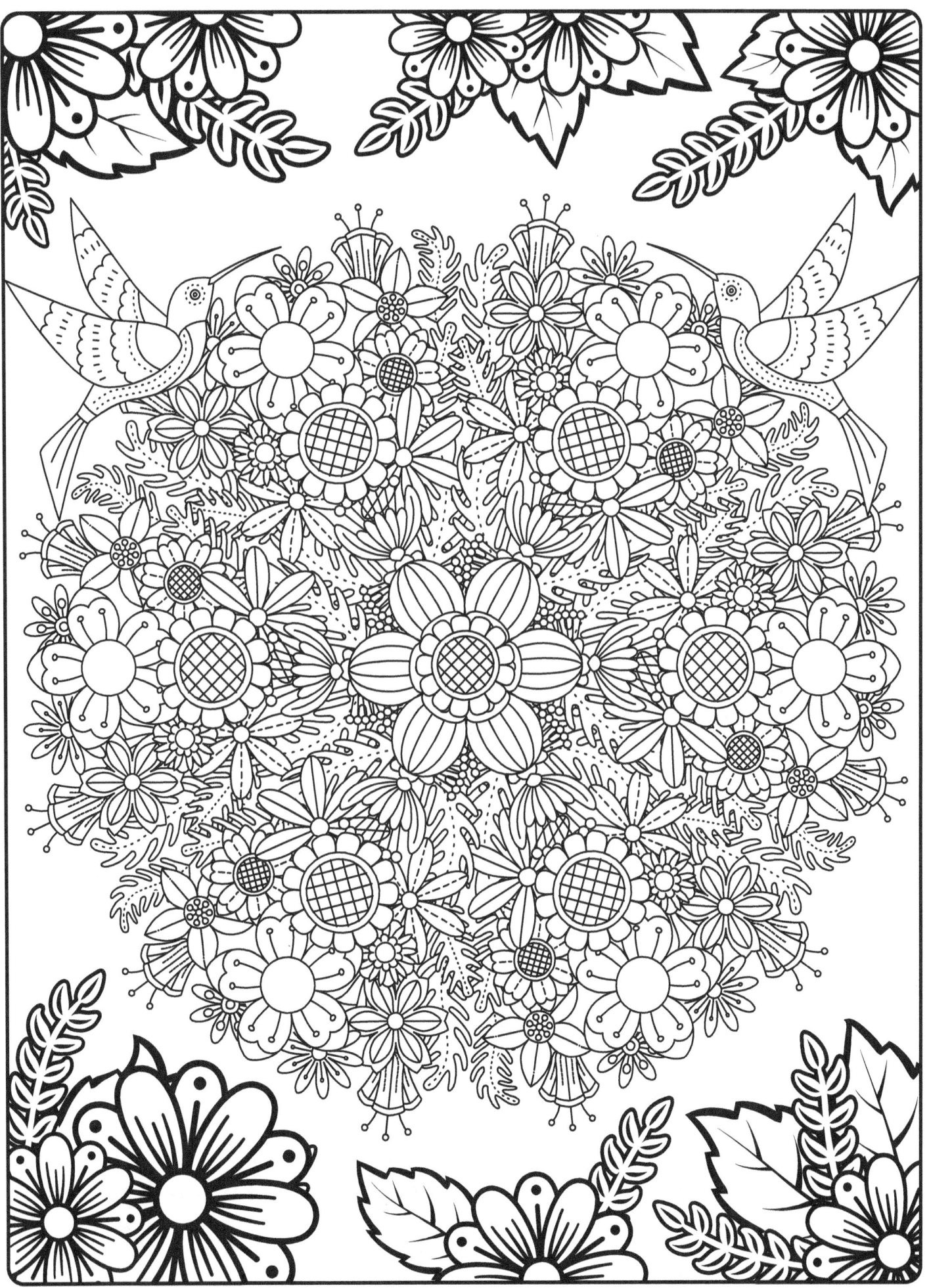

Reverse Mandala

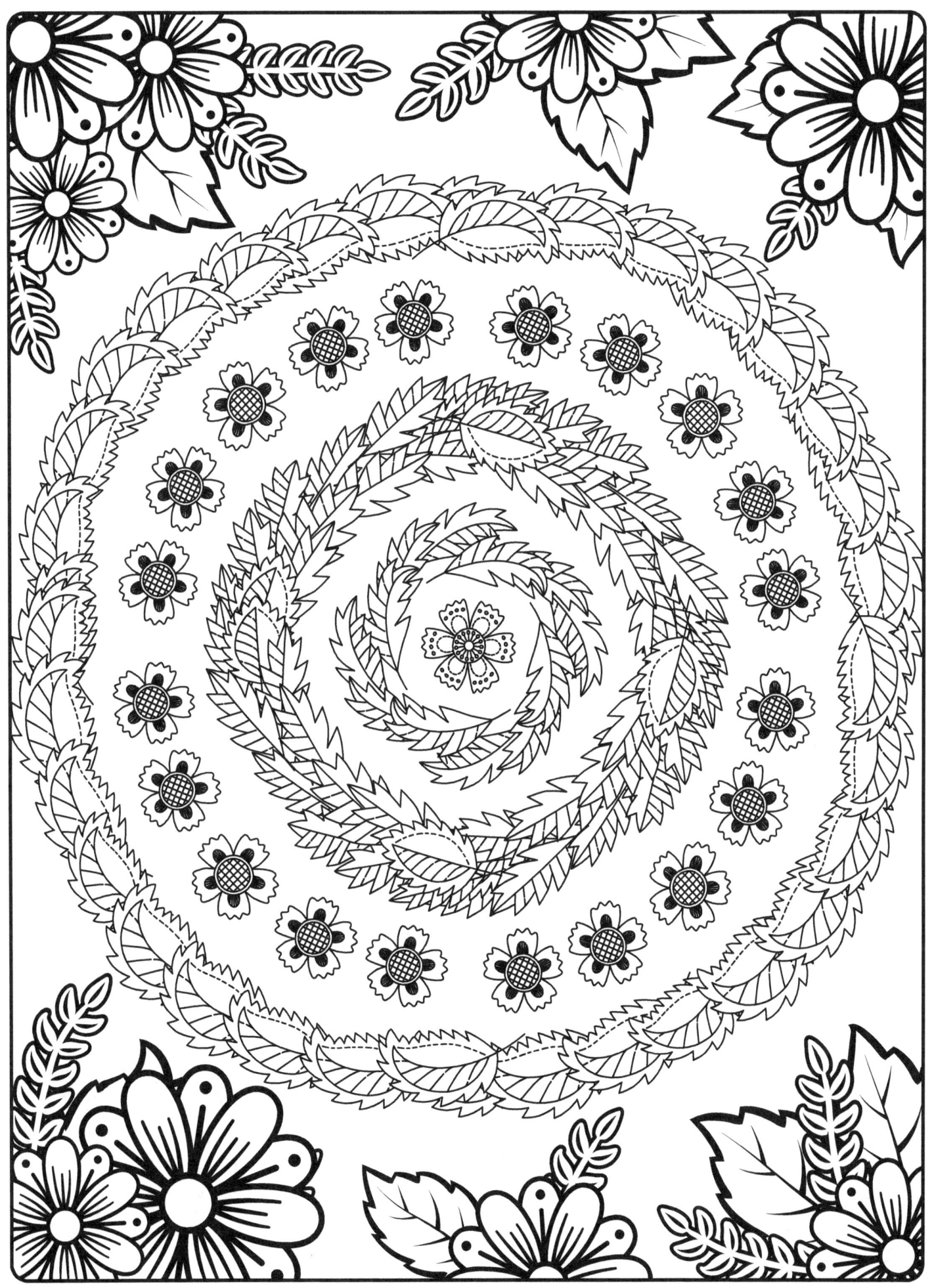

Reverse Mandala

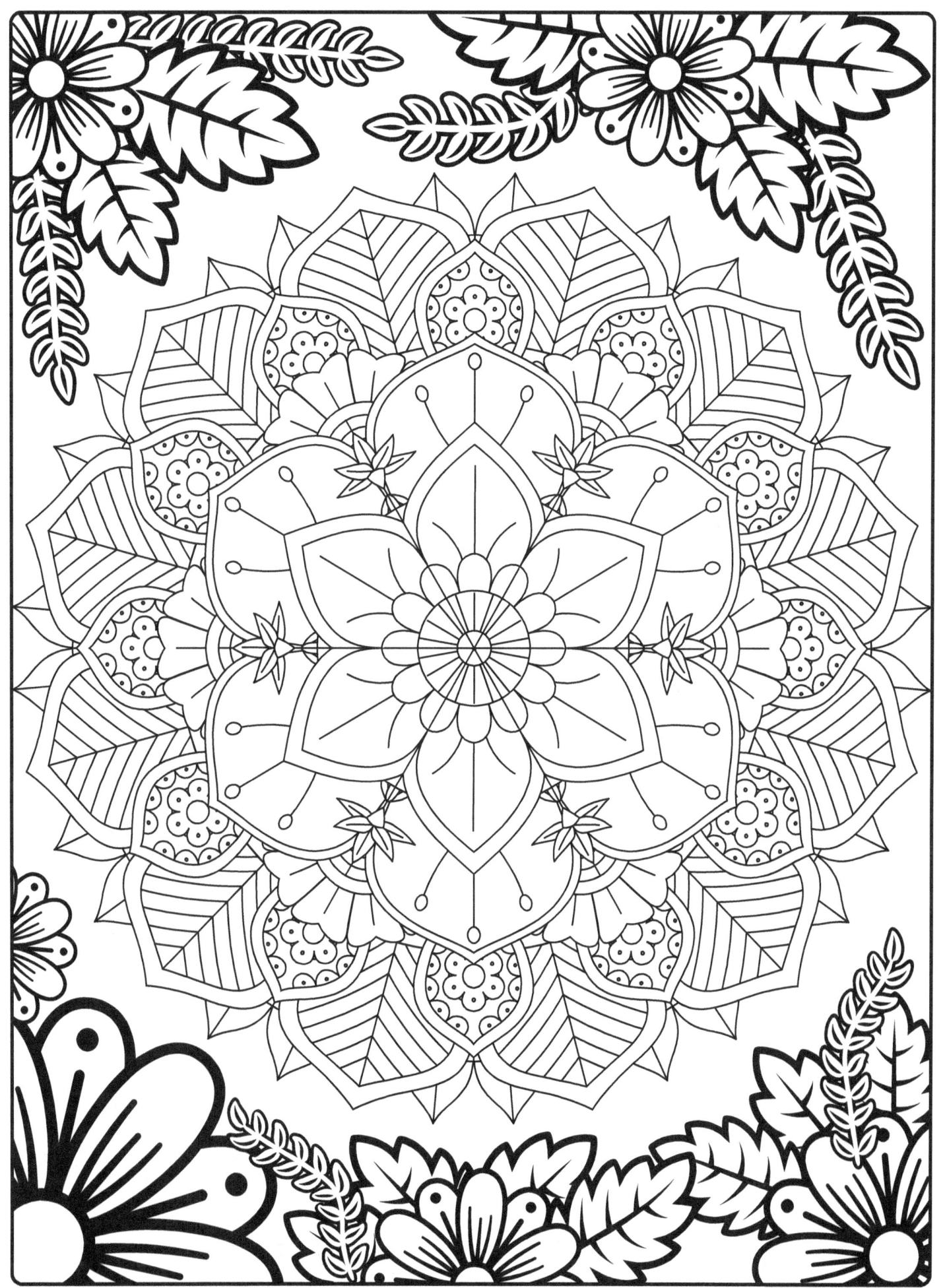

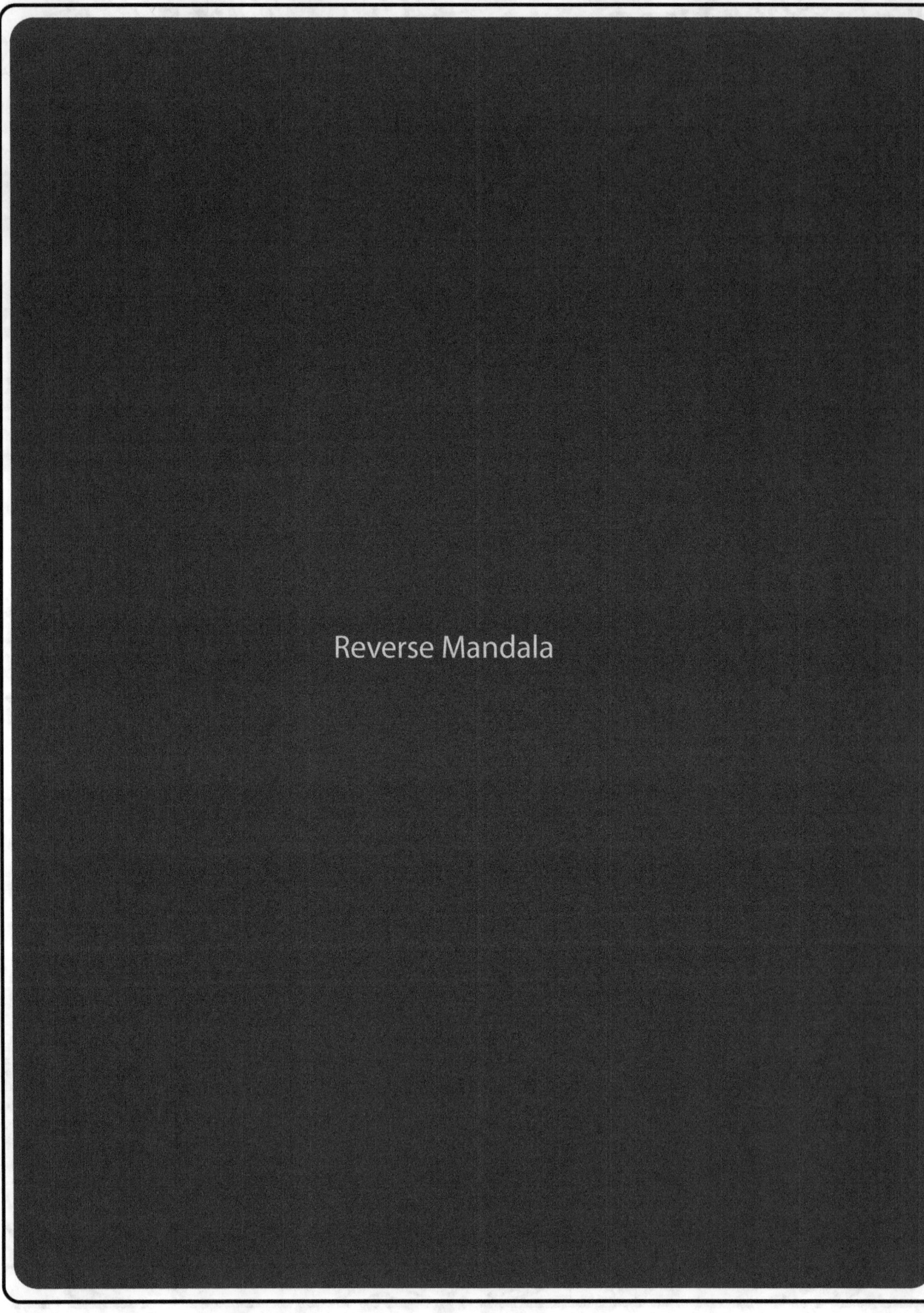

Reverse Mandala

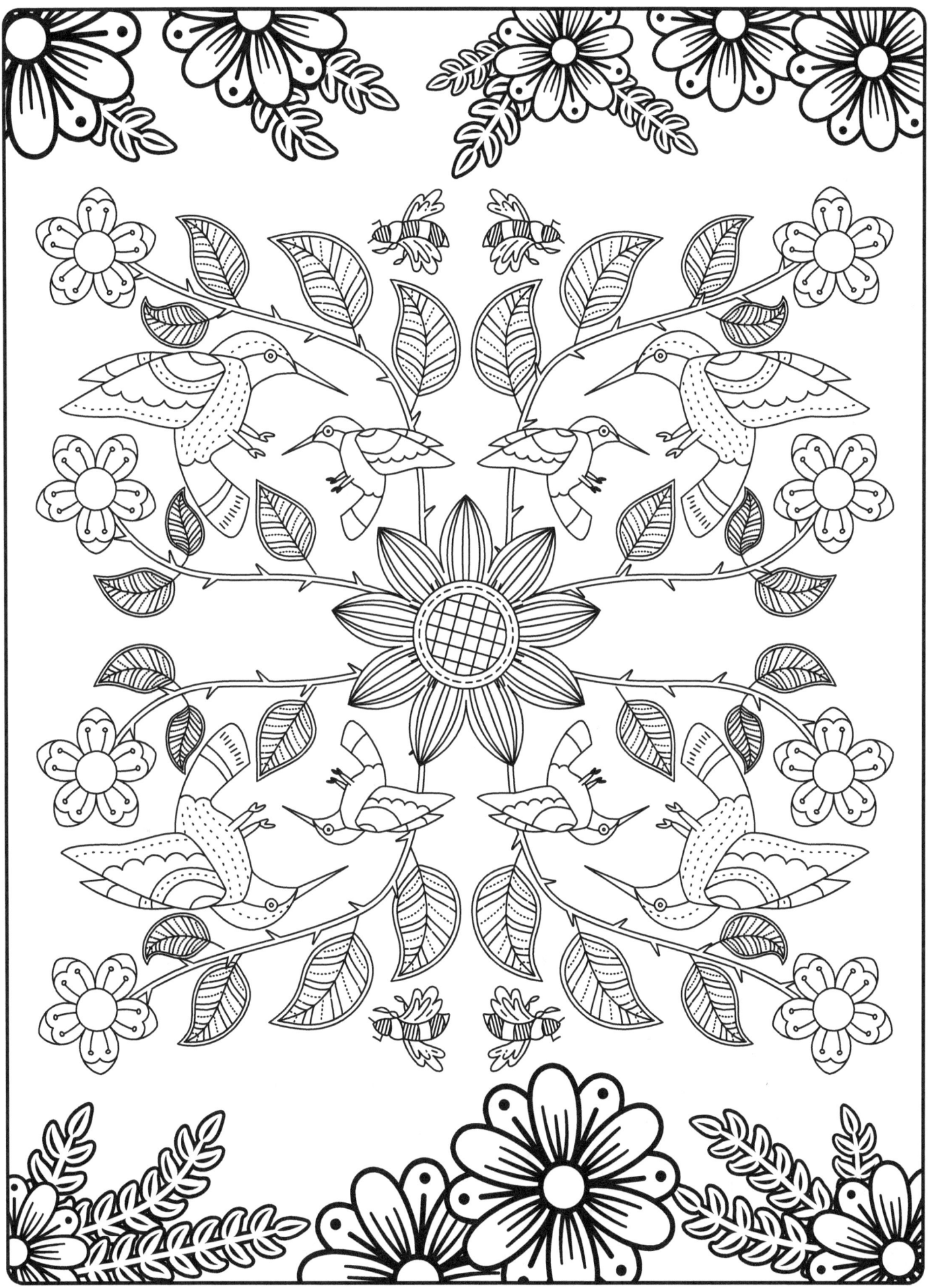

Reverse Mandala

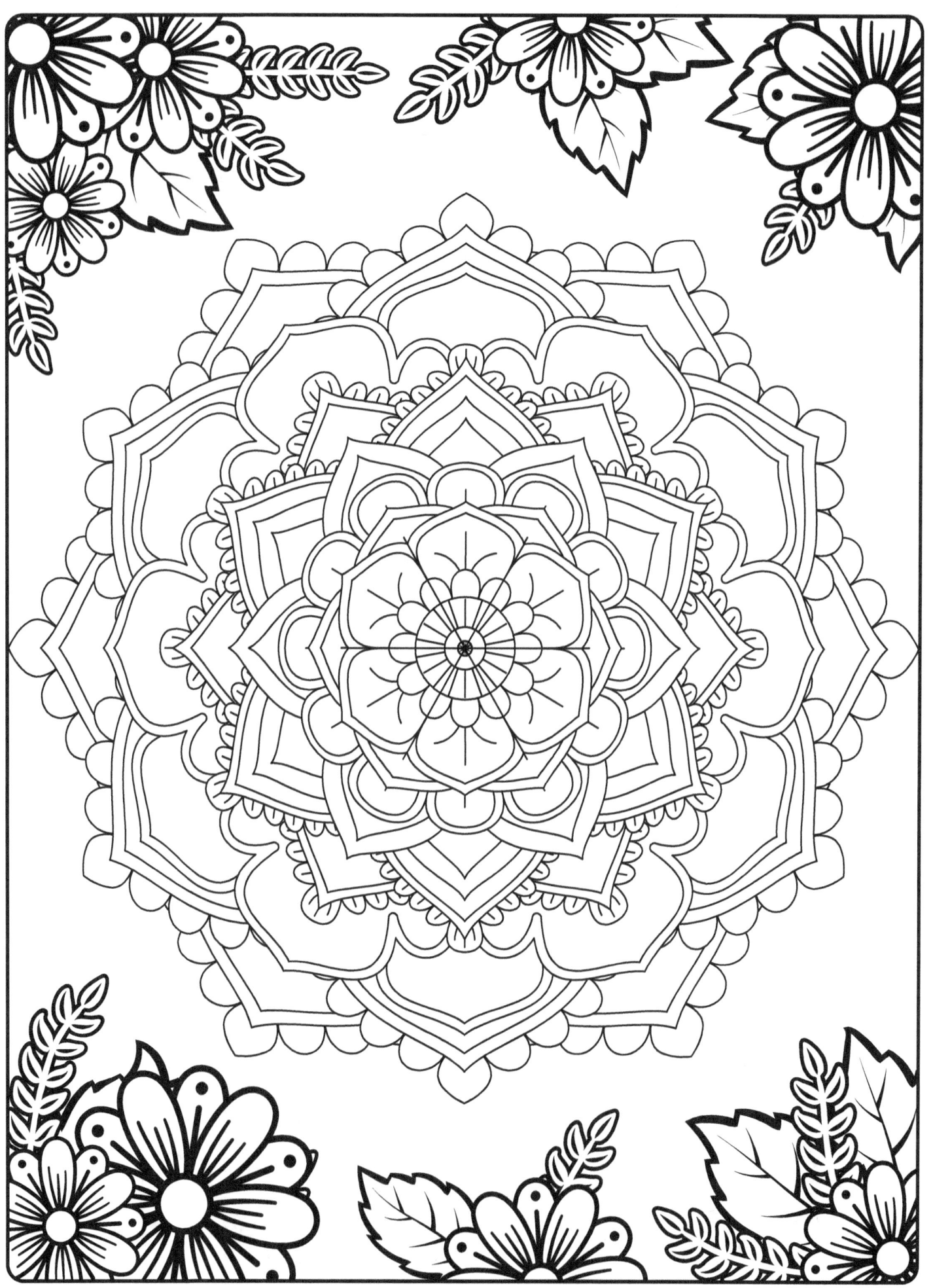

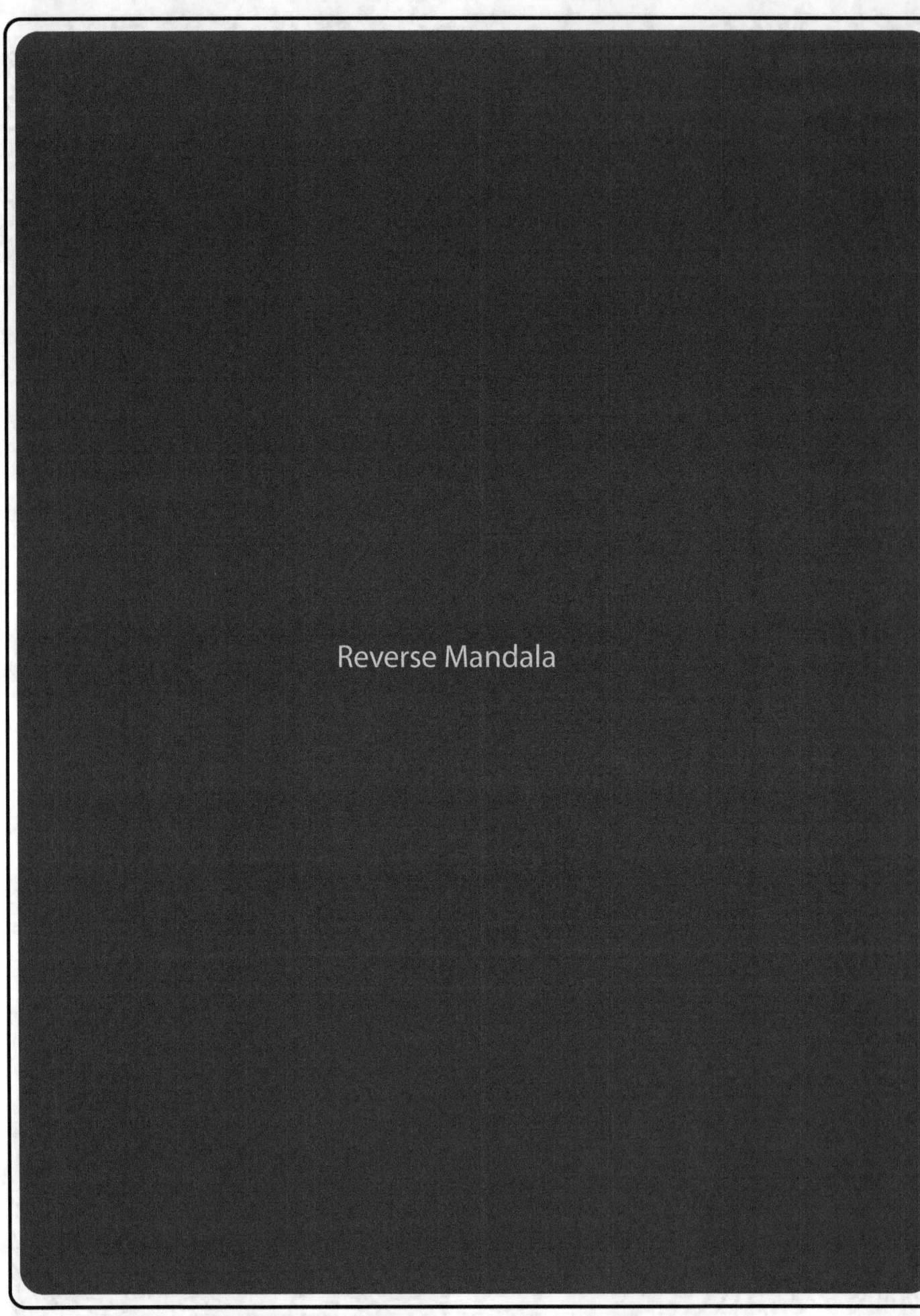

Reverse Mandala

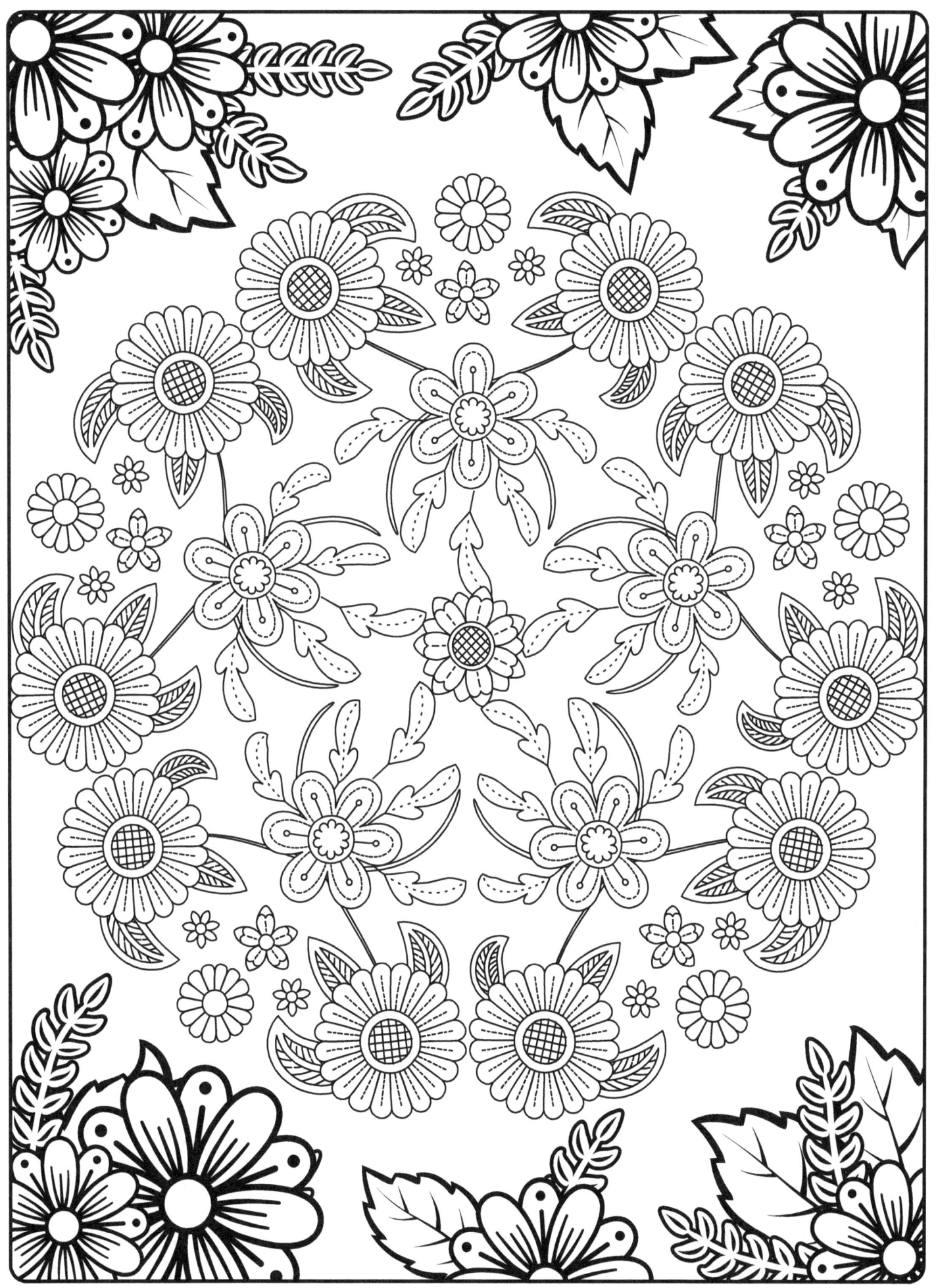

Reverse Mandala

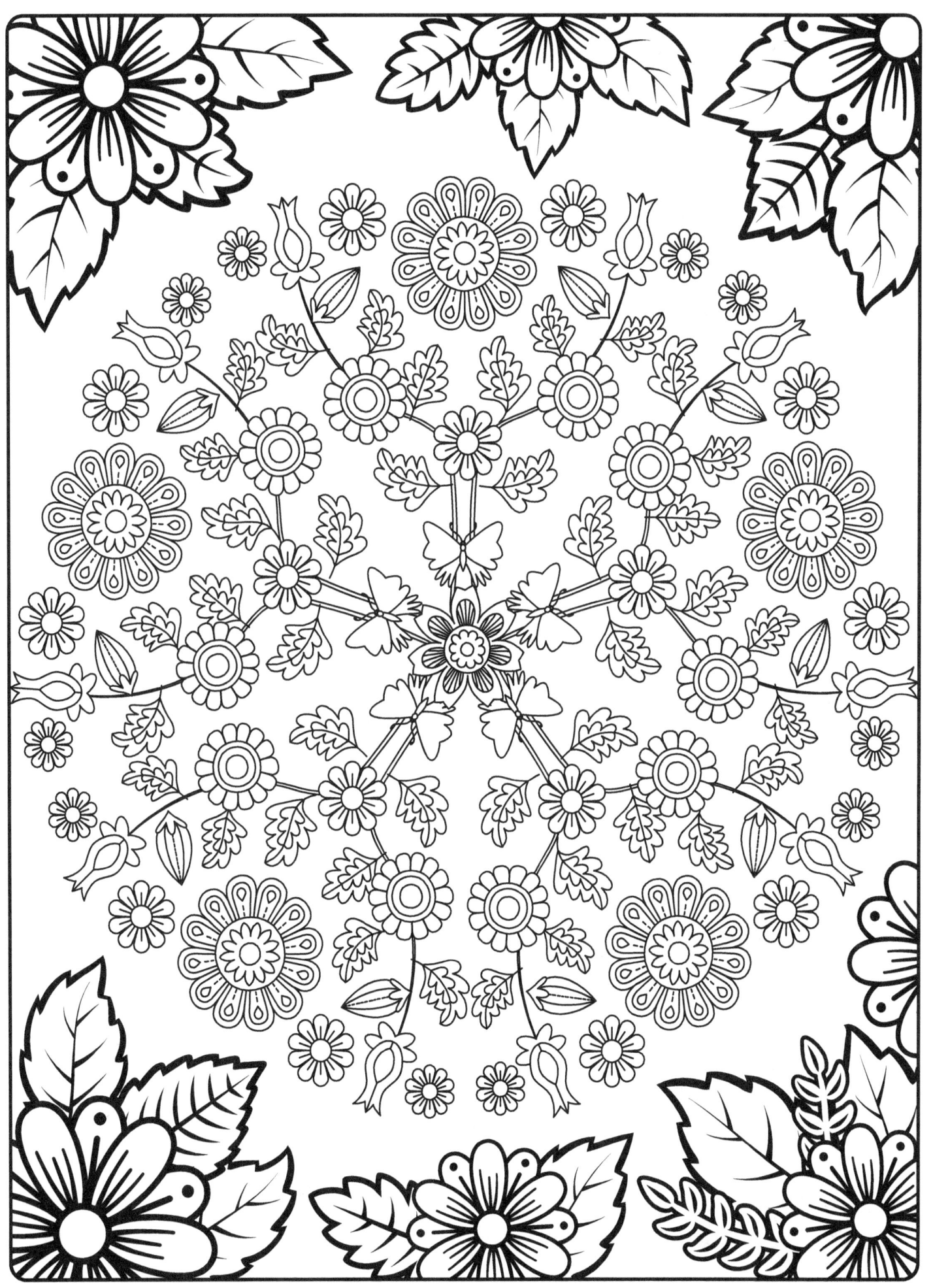

Reverse Mandala

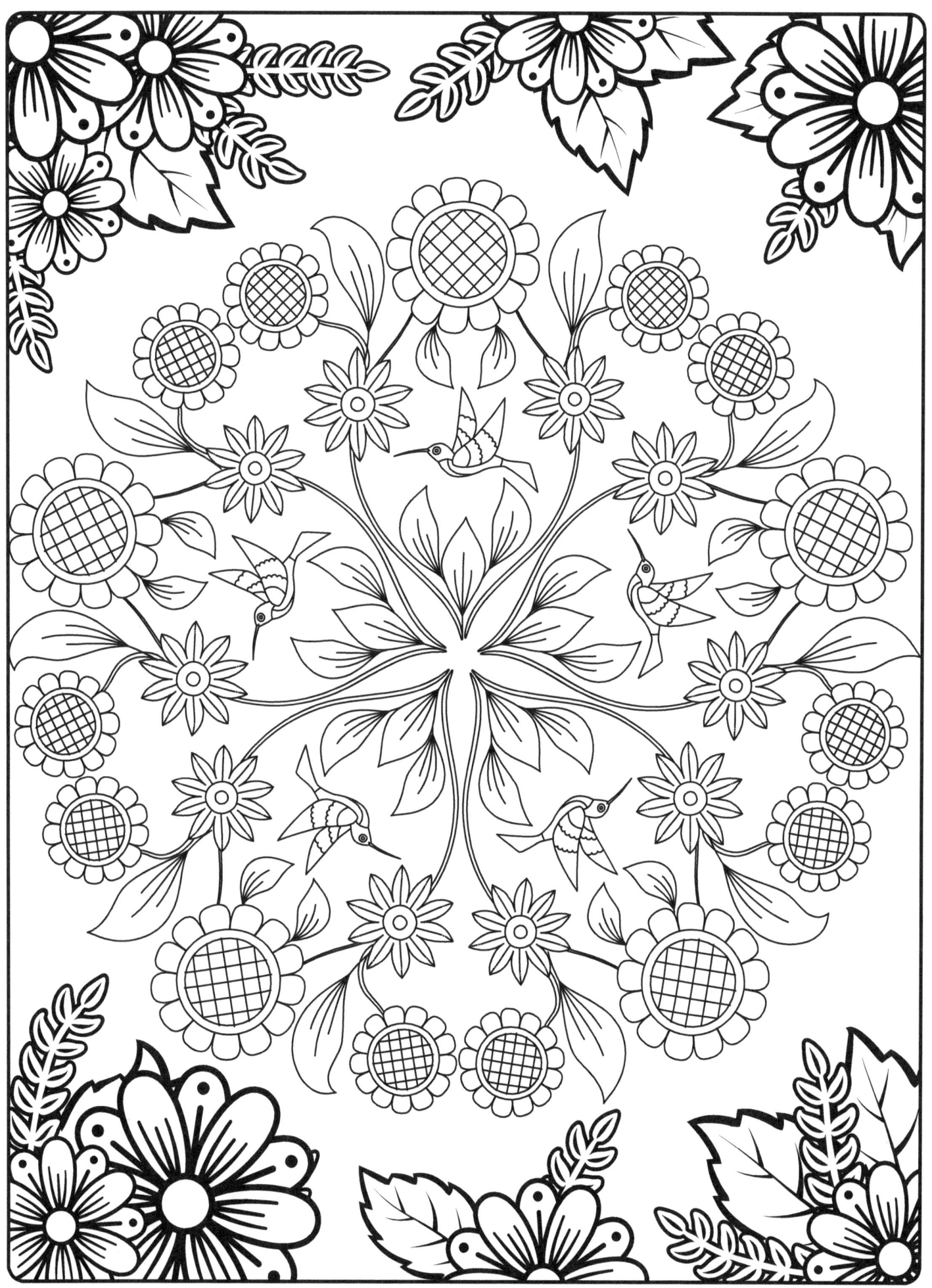

Reverse Mandala

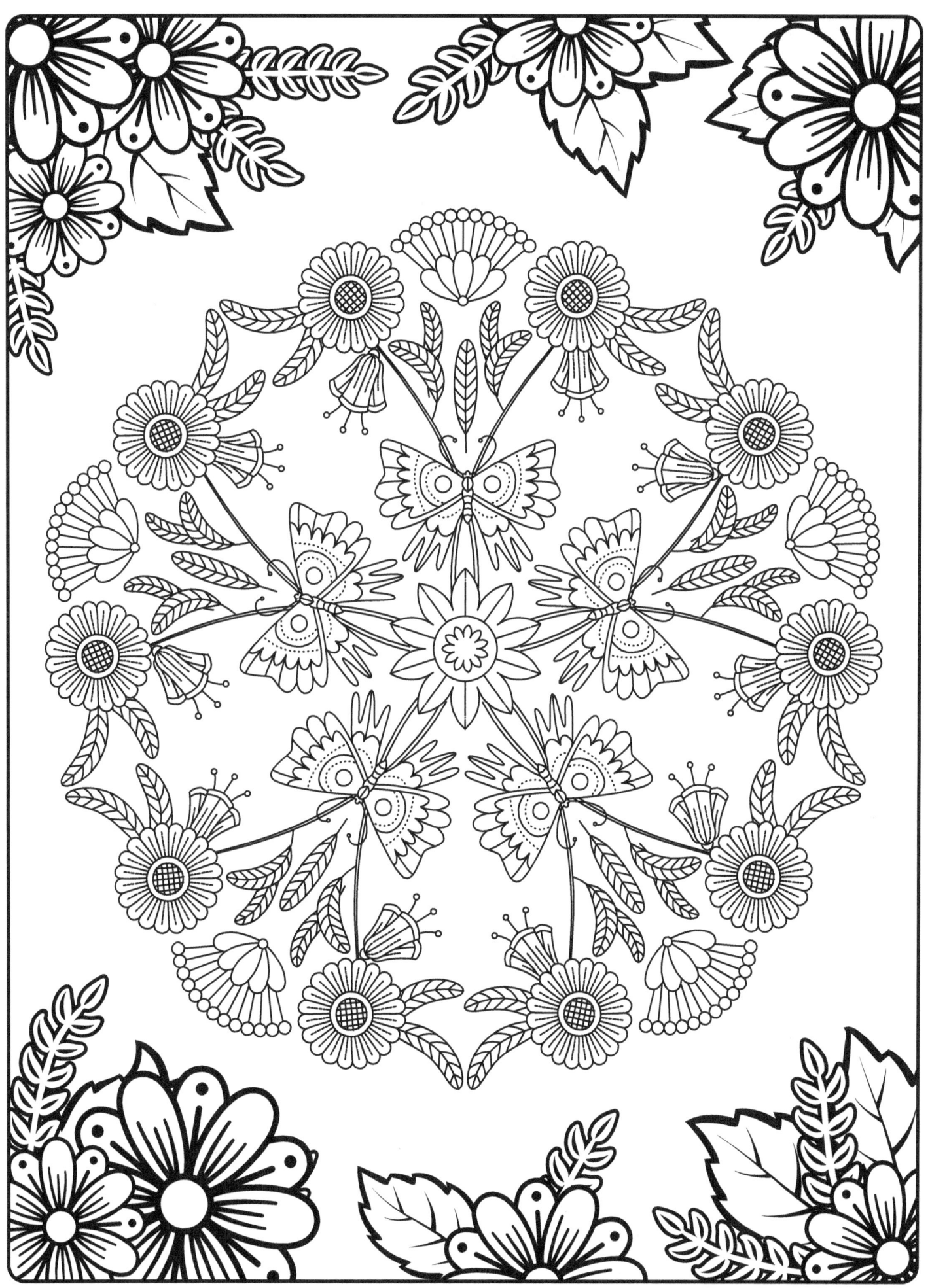

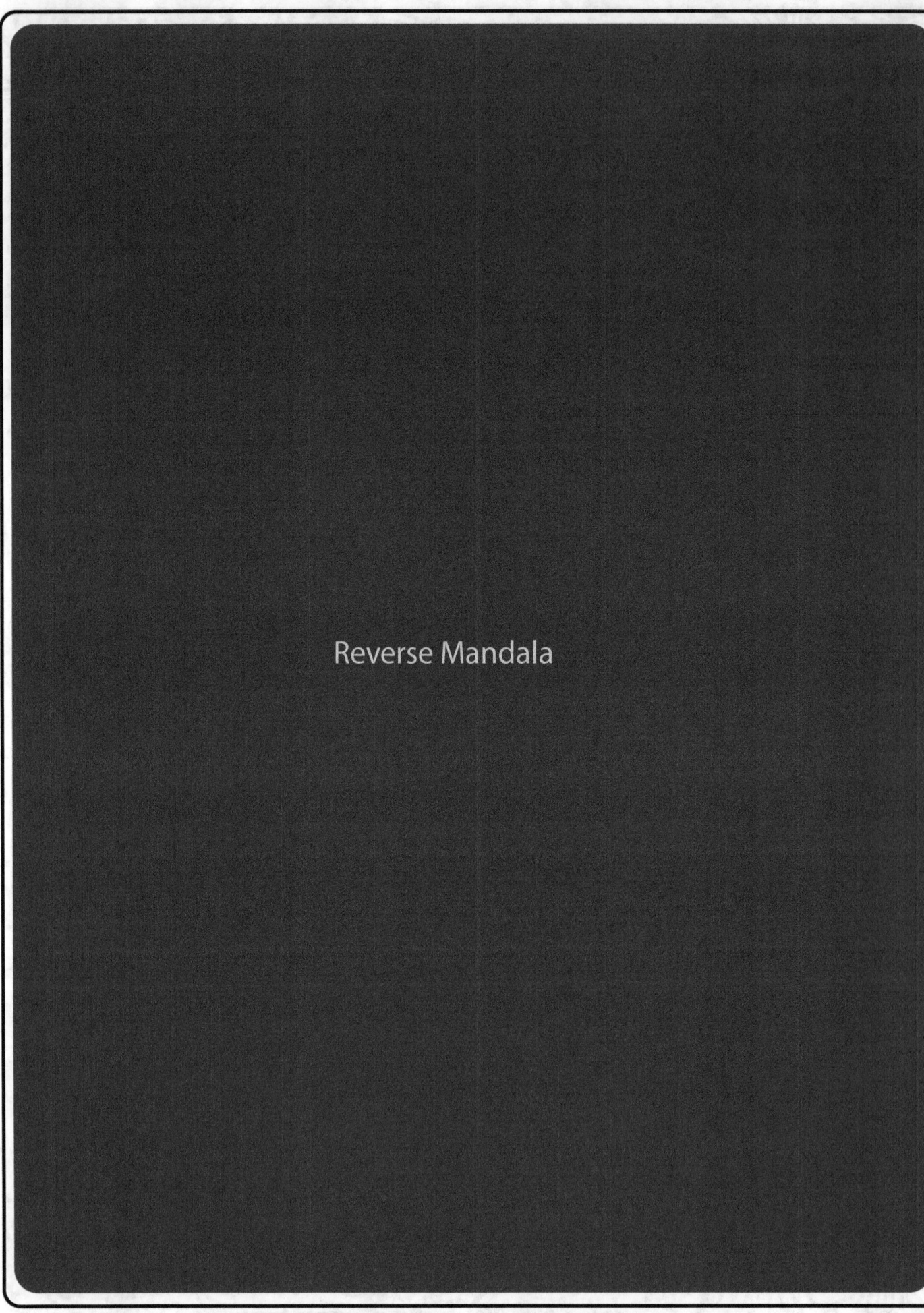

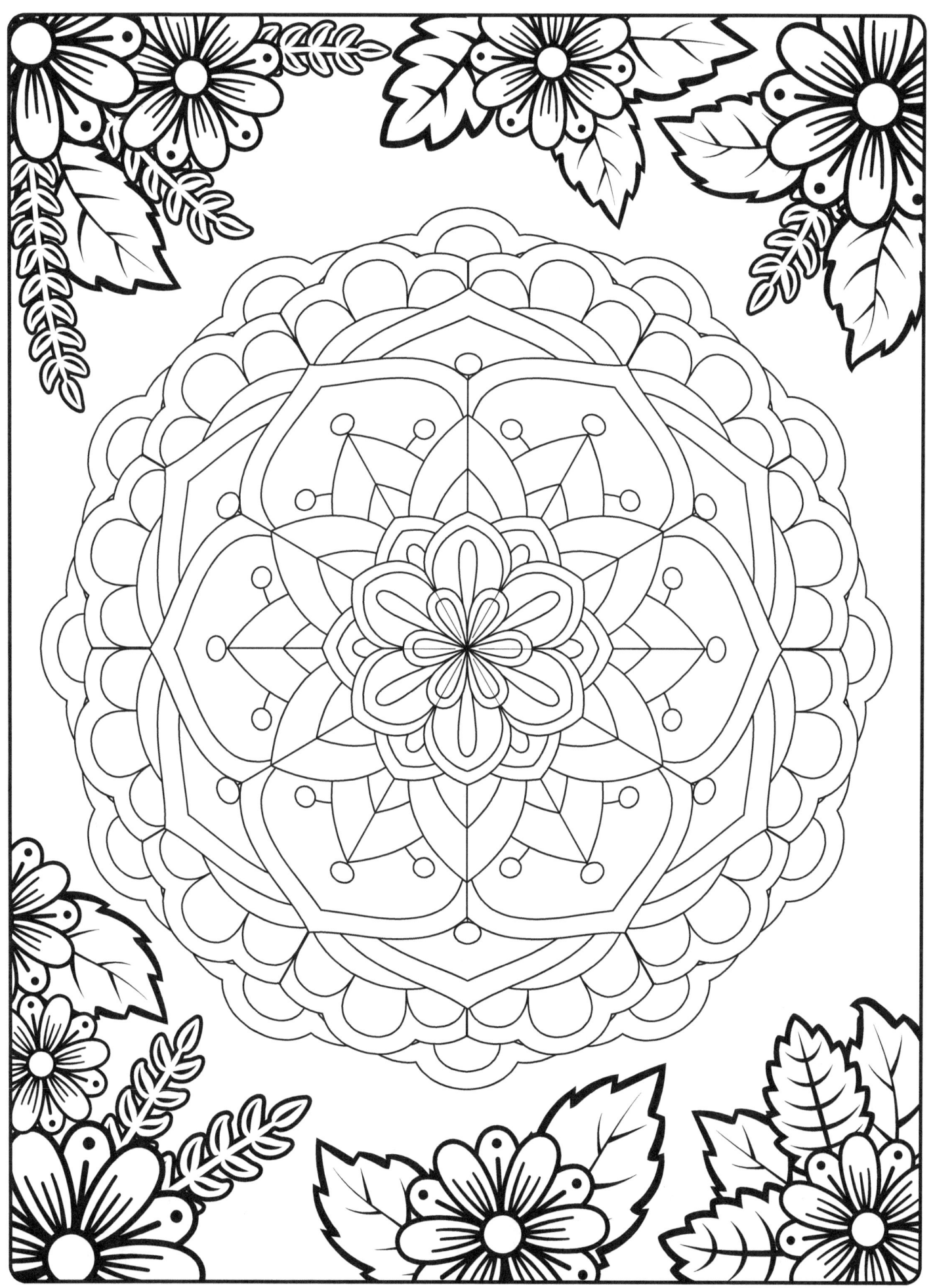

Reverse Mandala

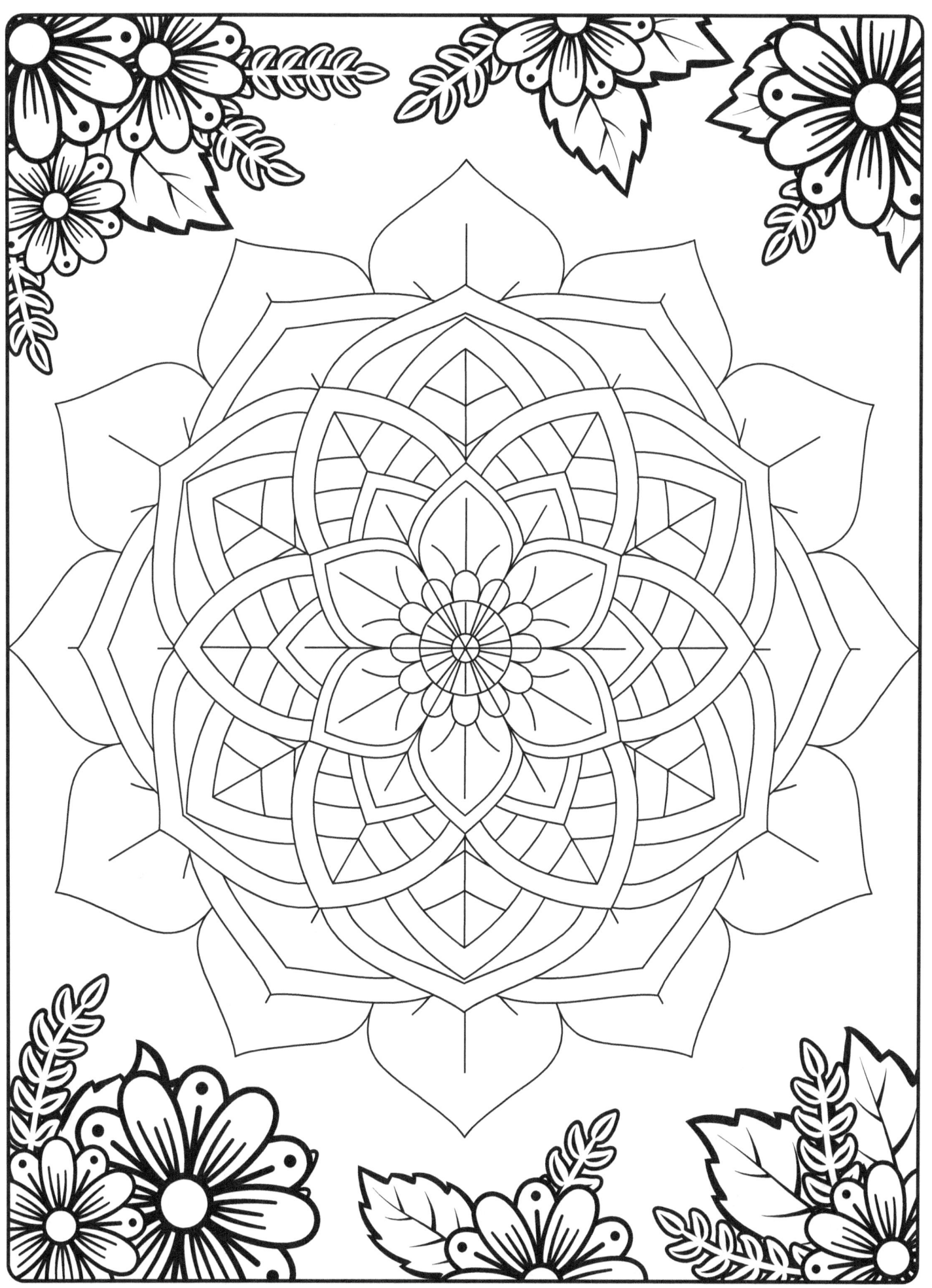

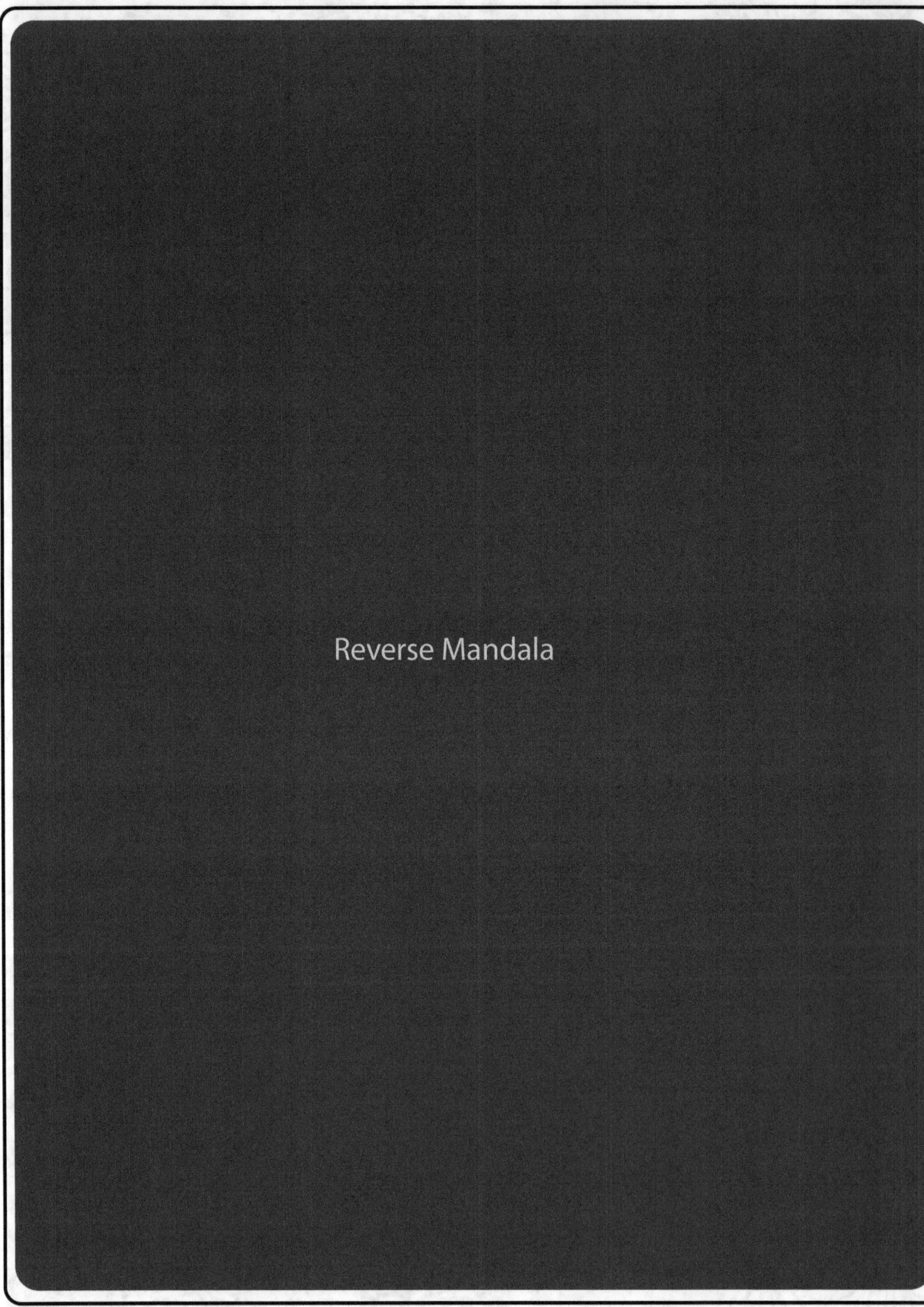
Reverse Mandala

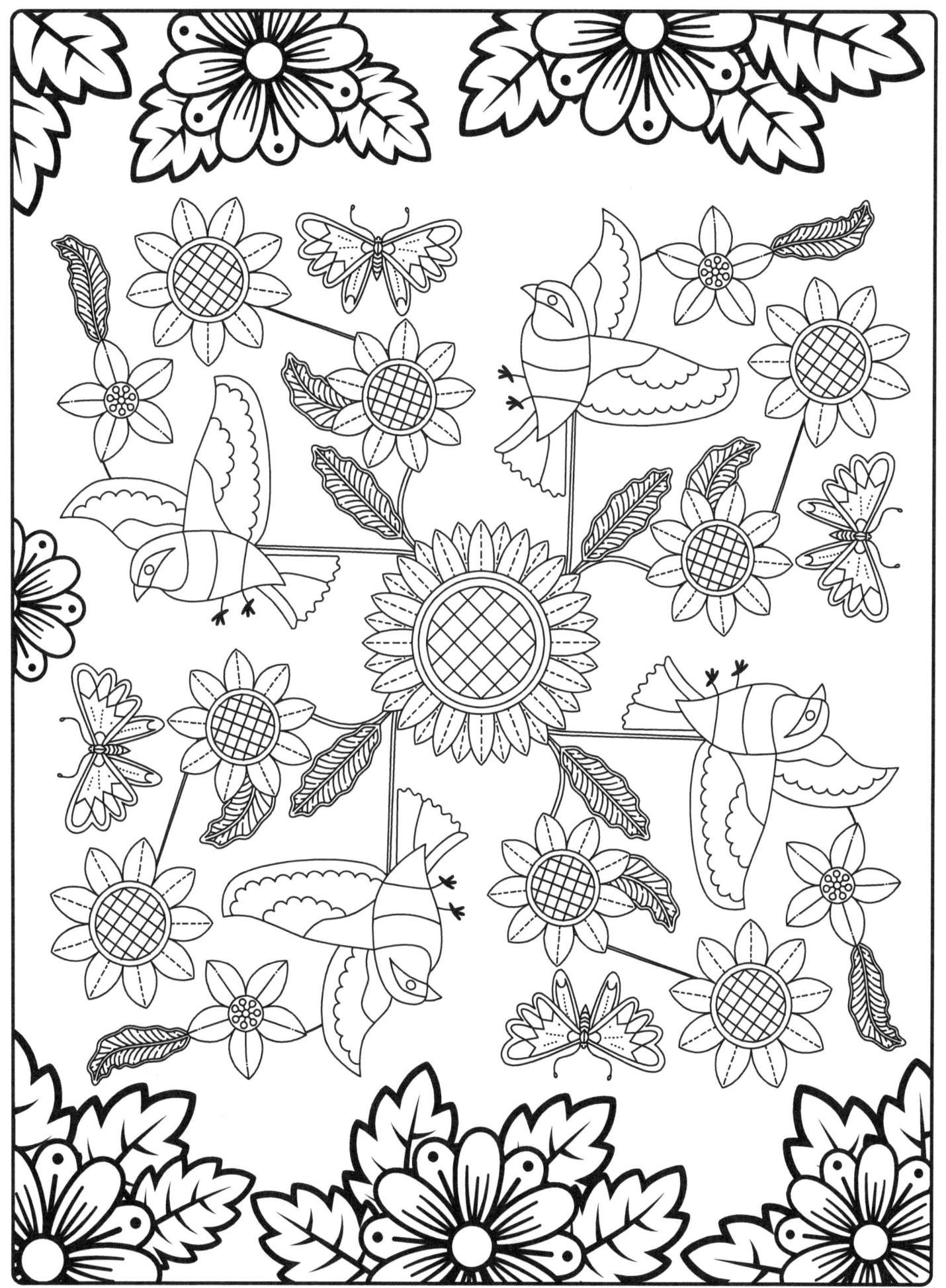

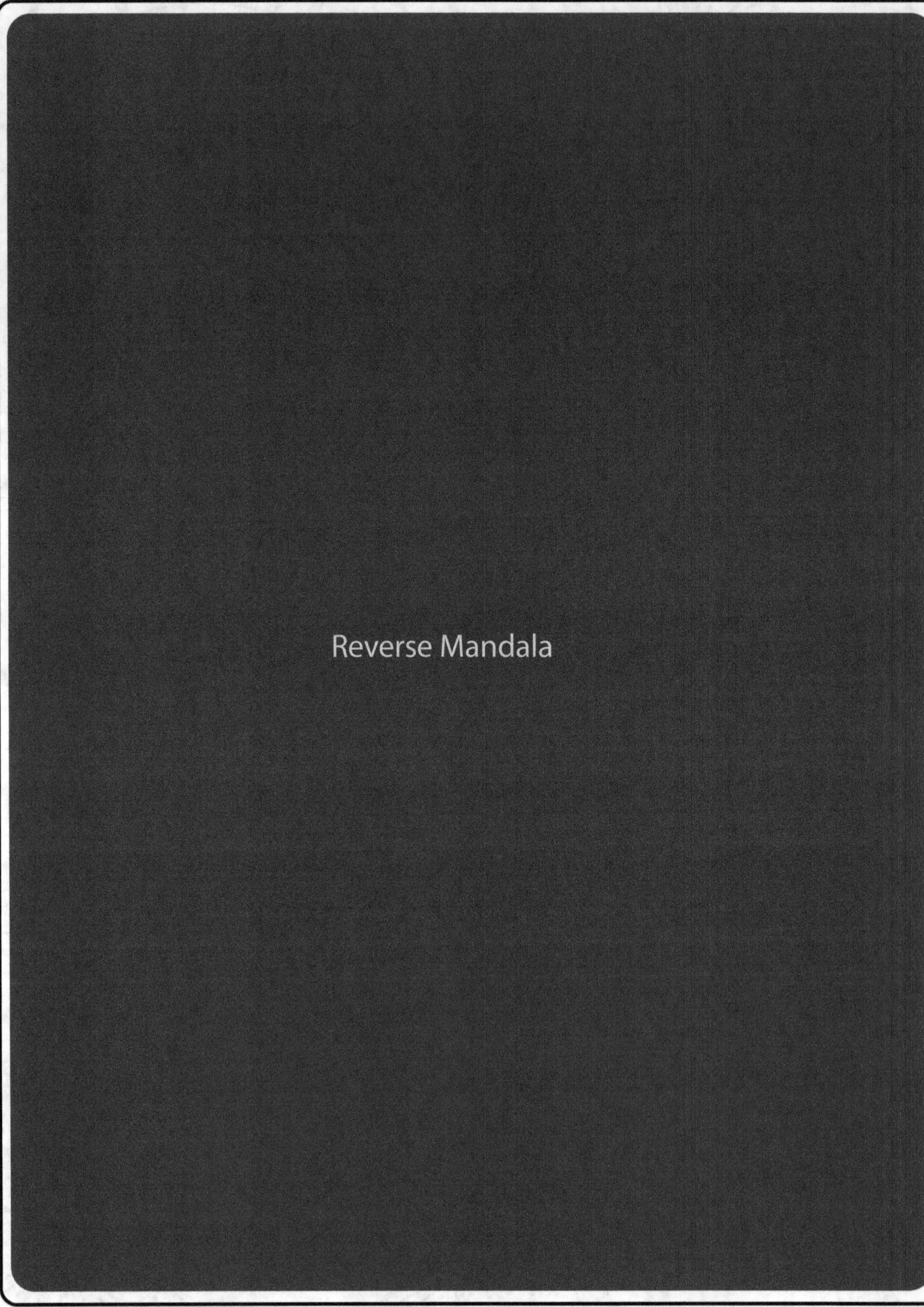
Reverse Mandala

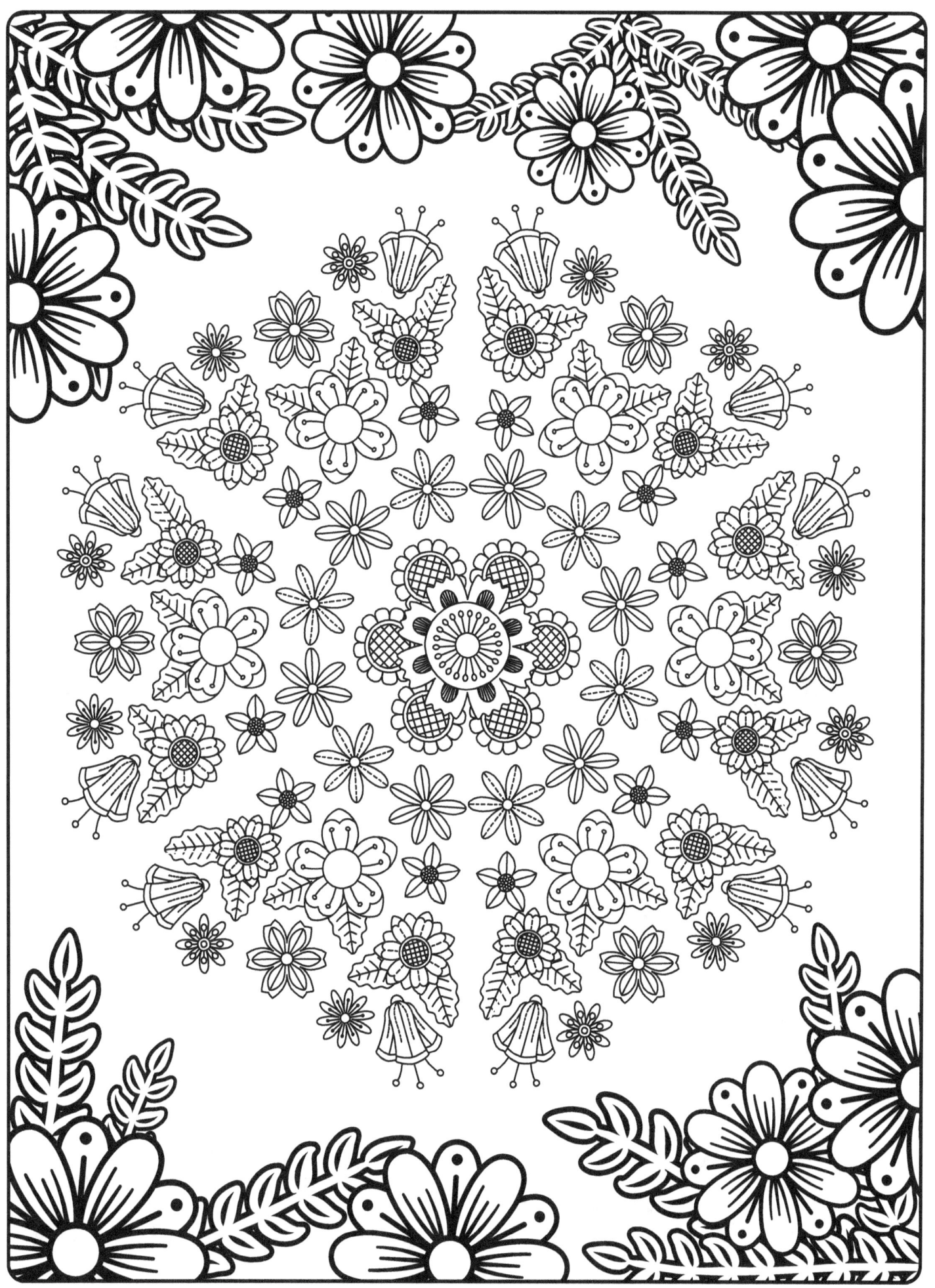

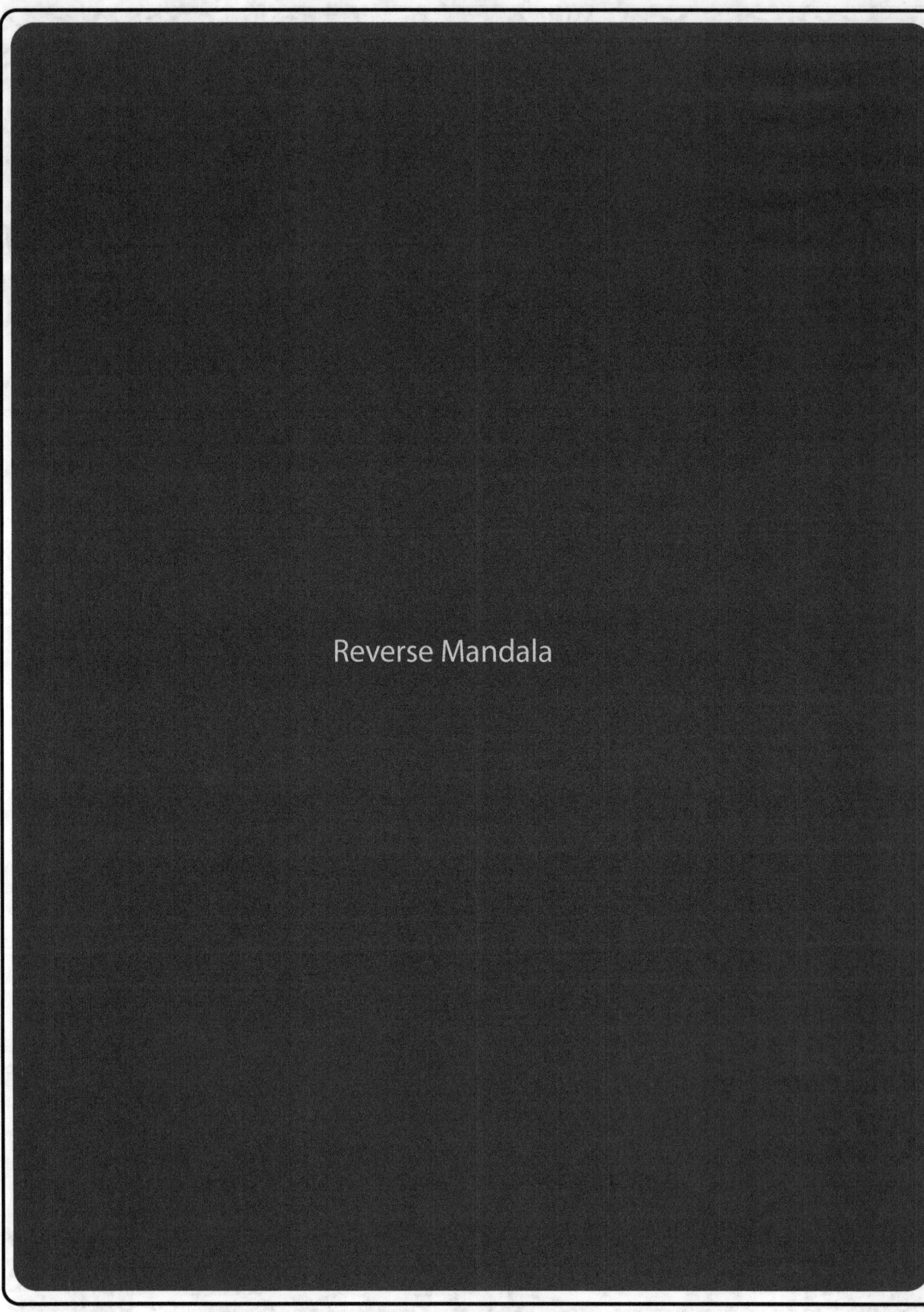

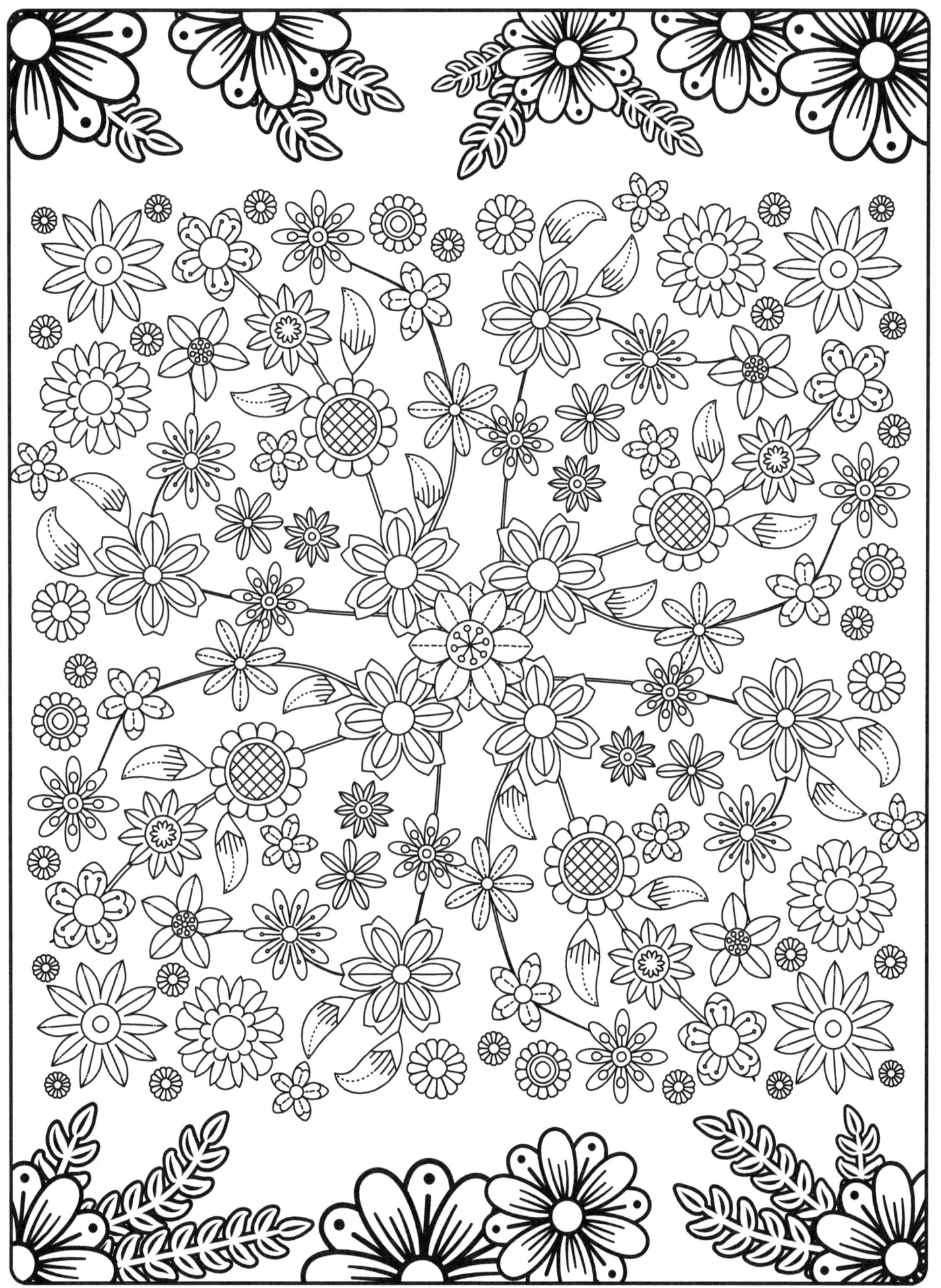

Reverse Mandala

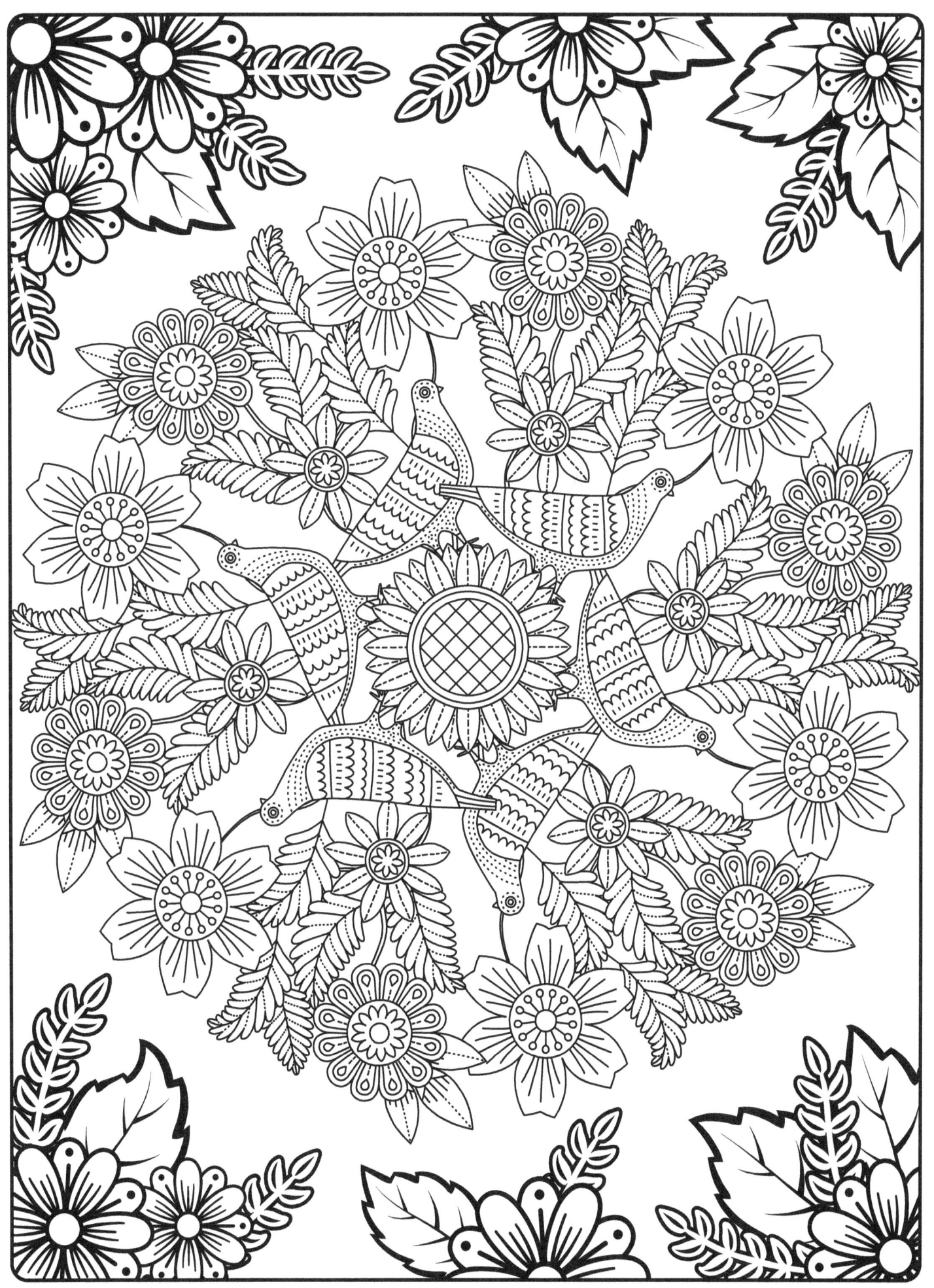

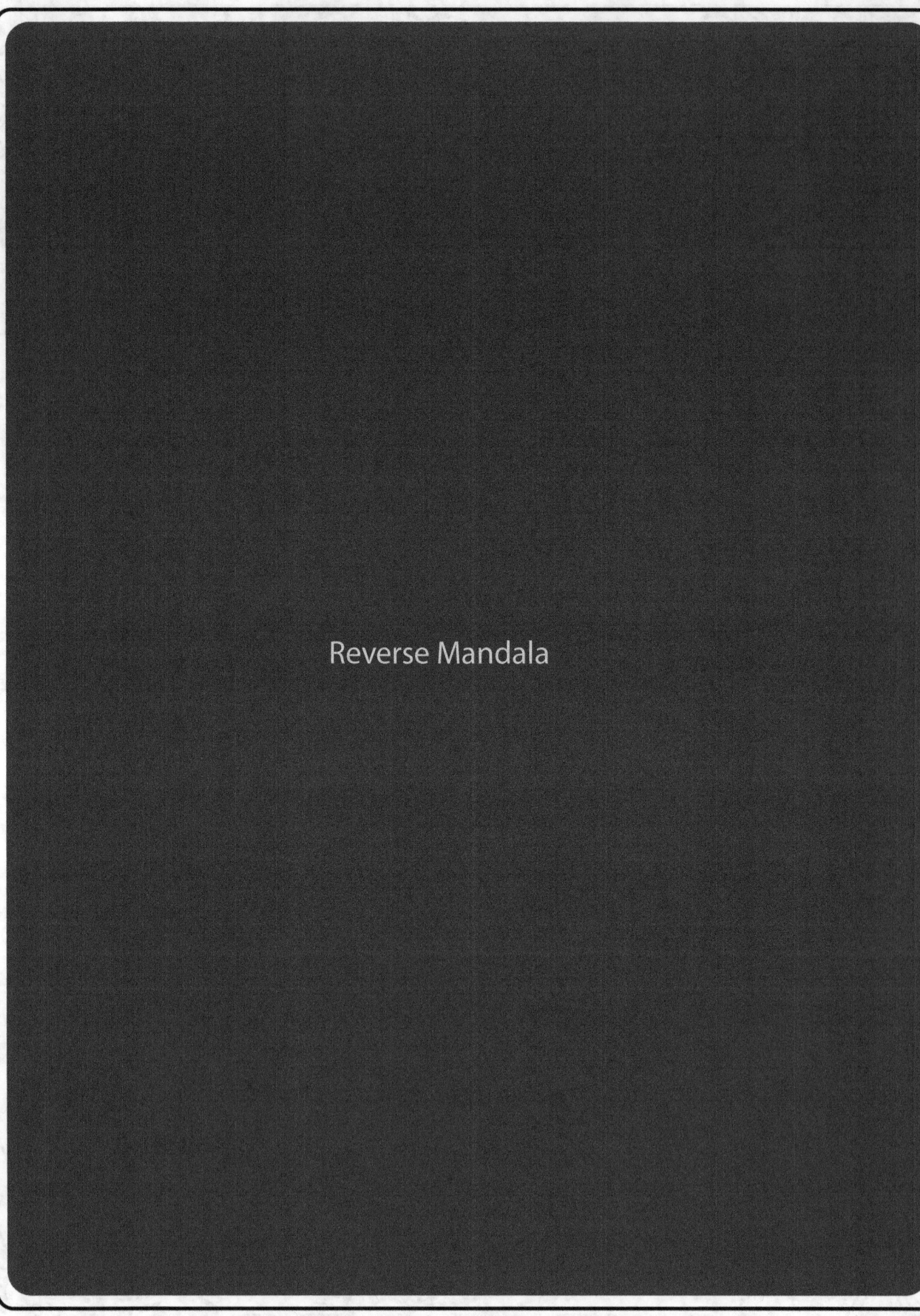

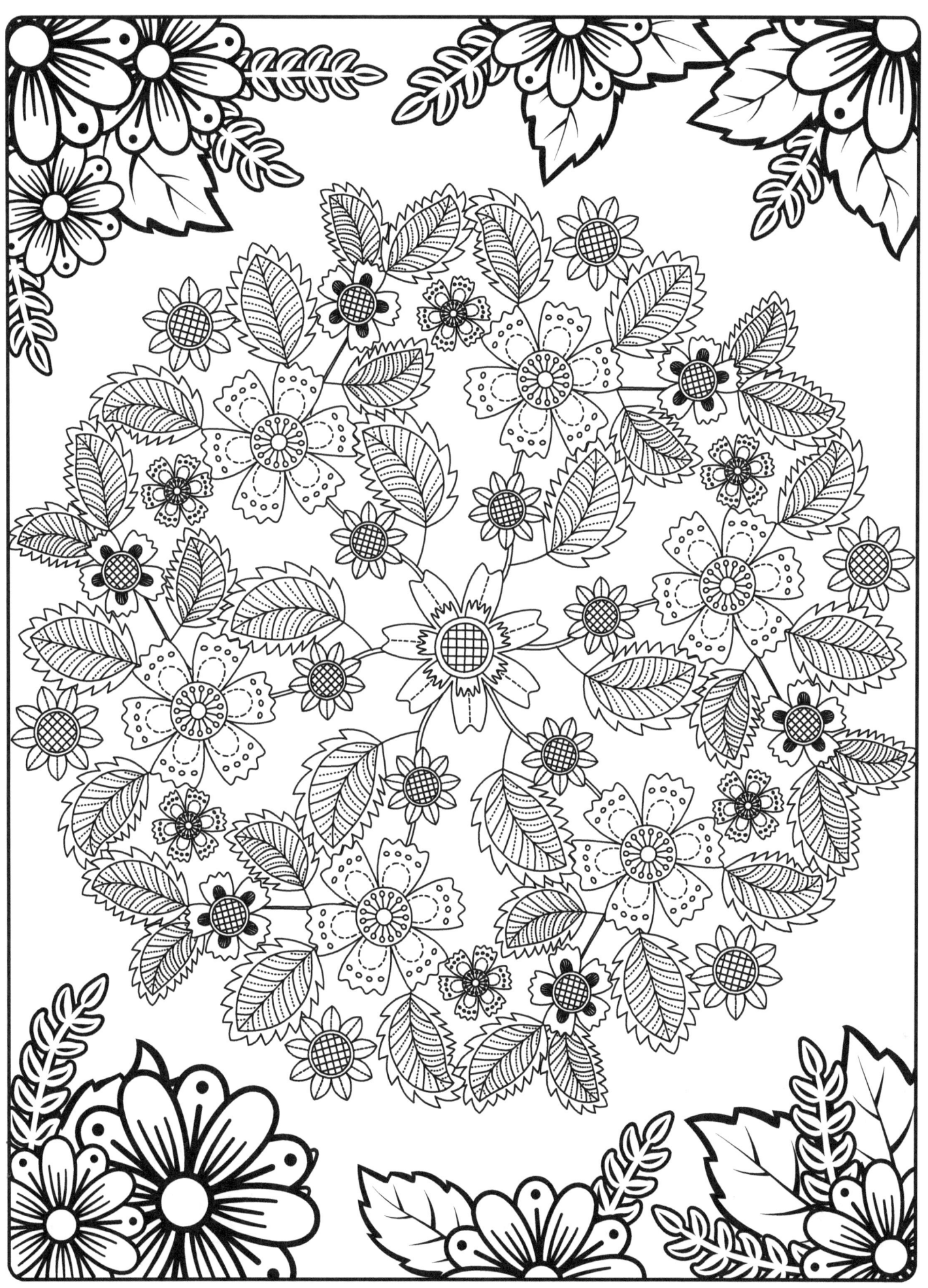

Reverse Mandala

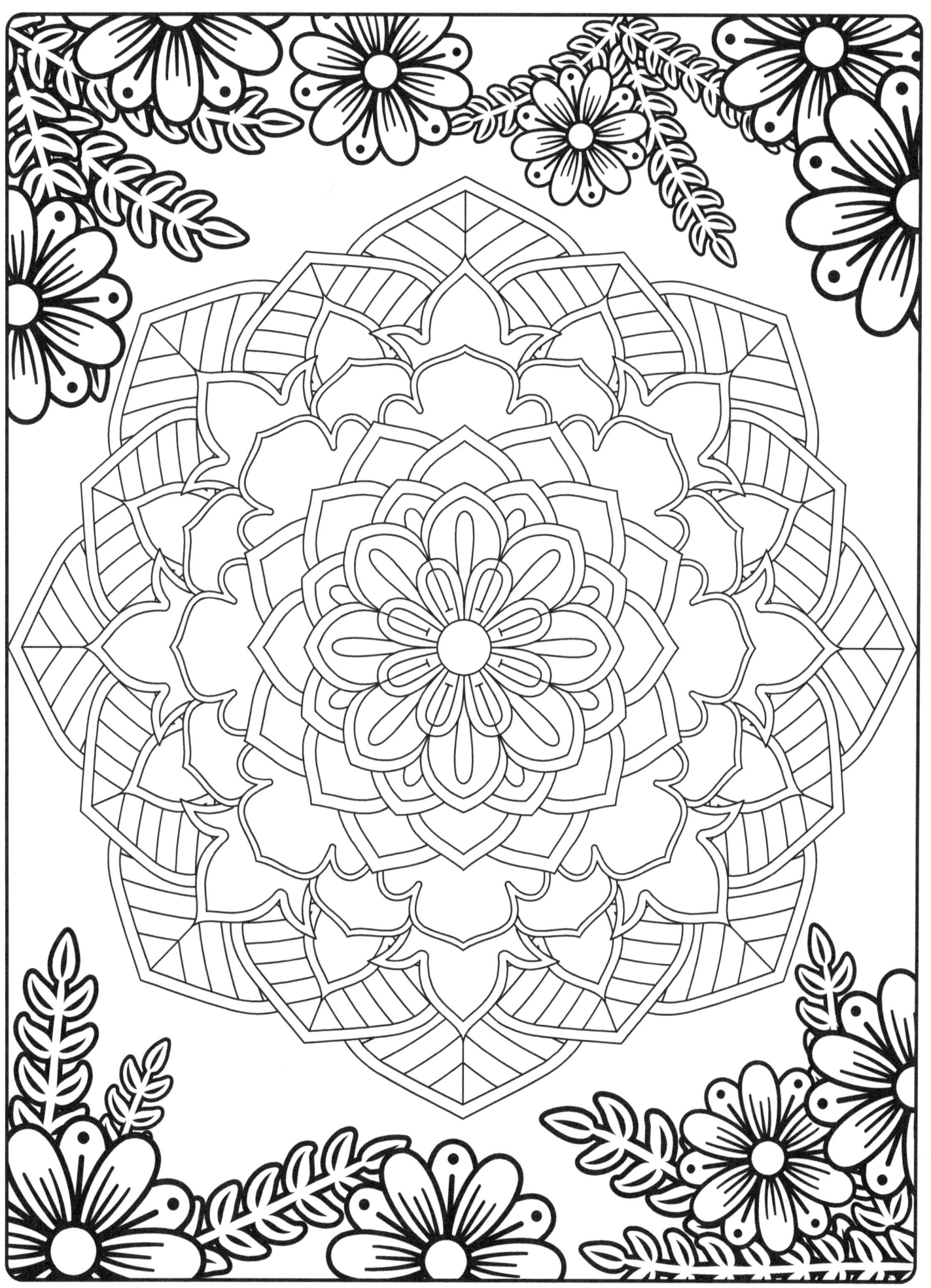

Reverse Mandala

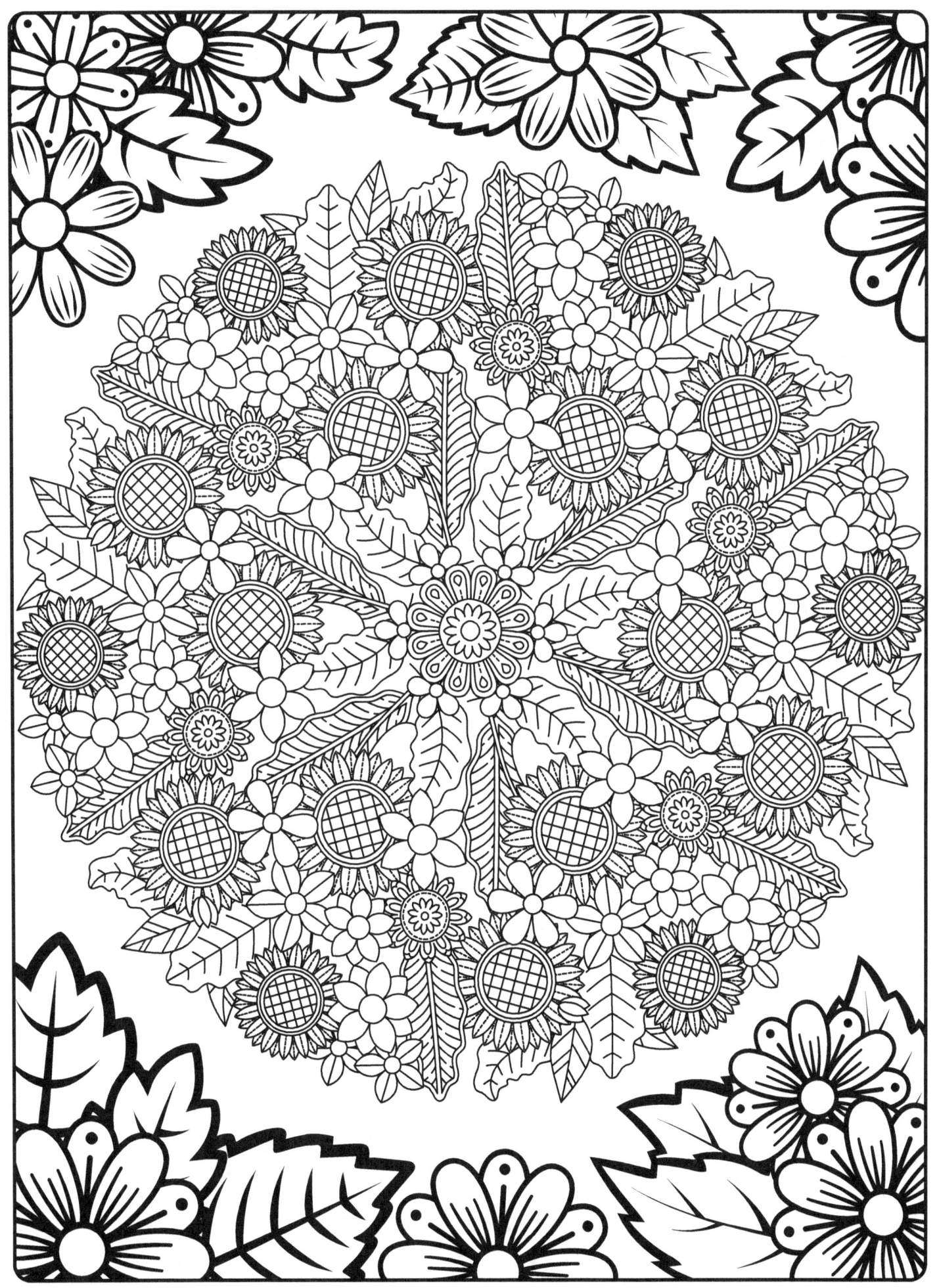

Reverse Mandala

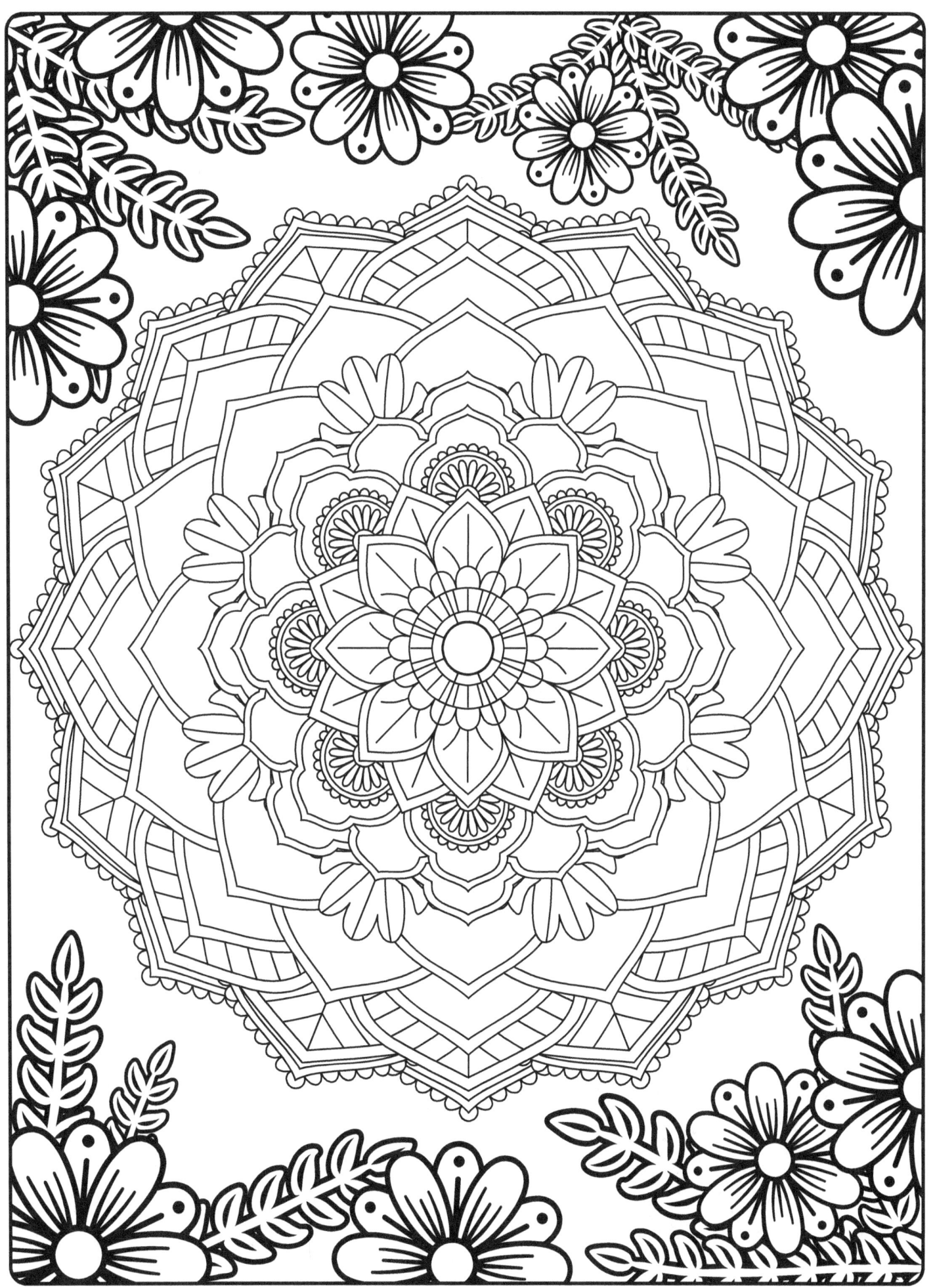

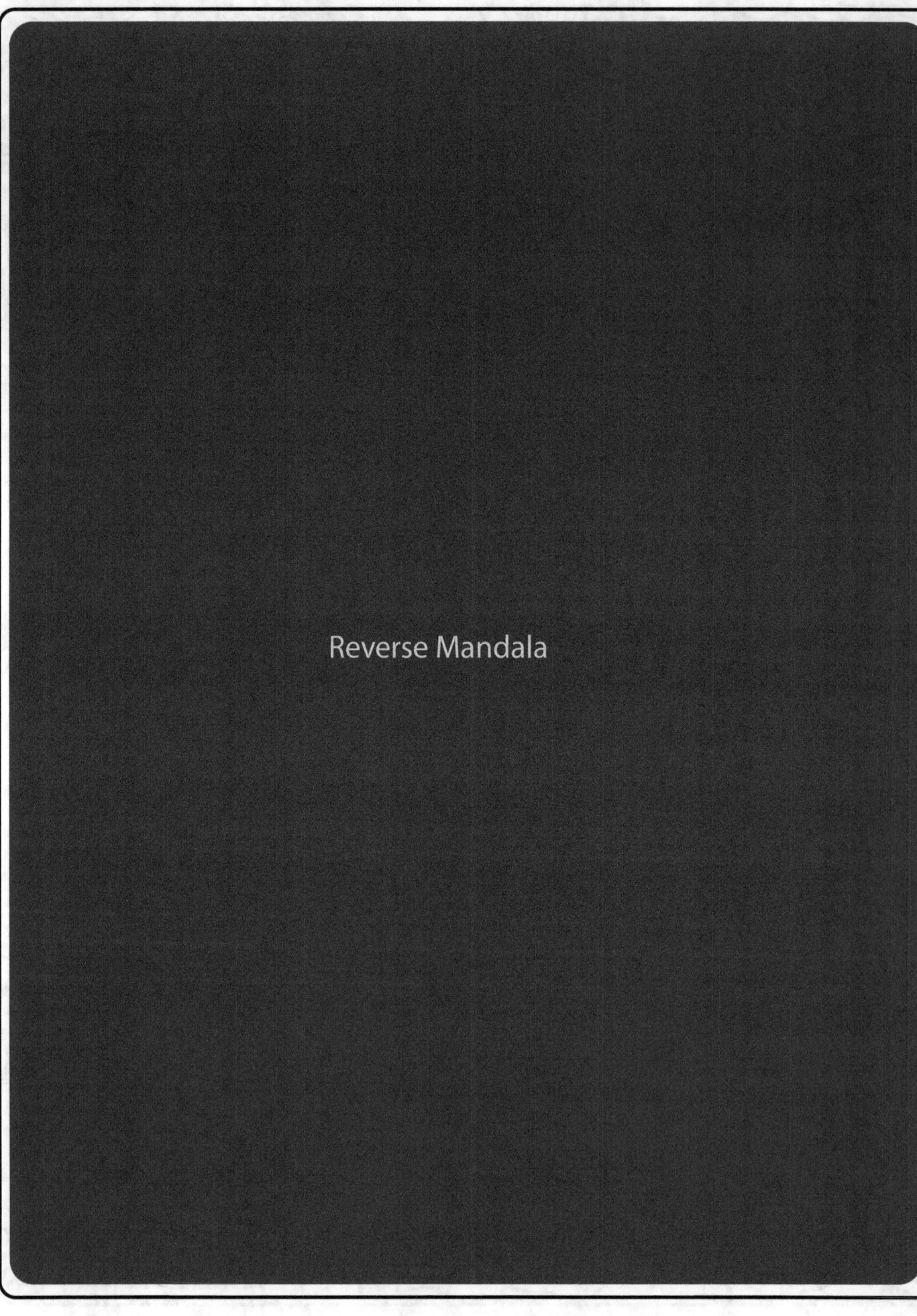
Reverse Mandala

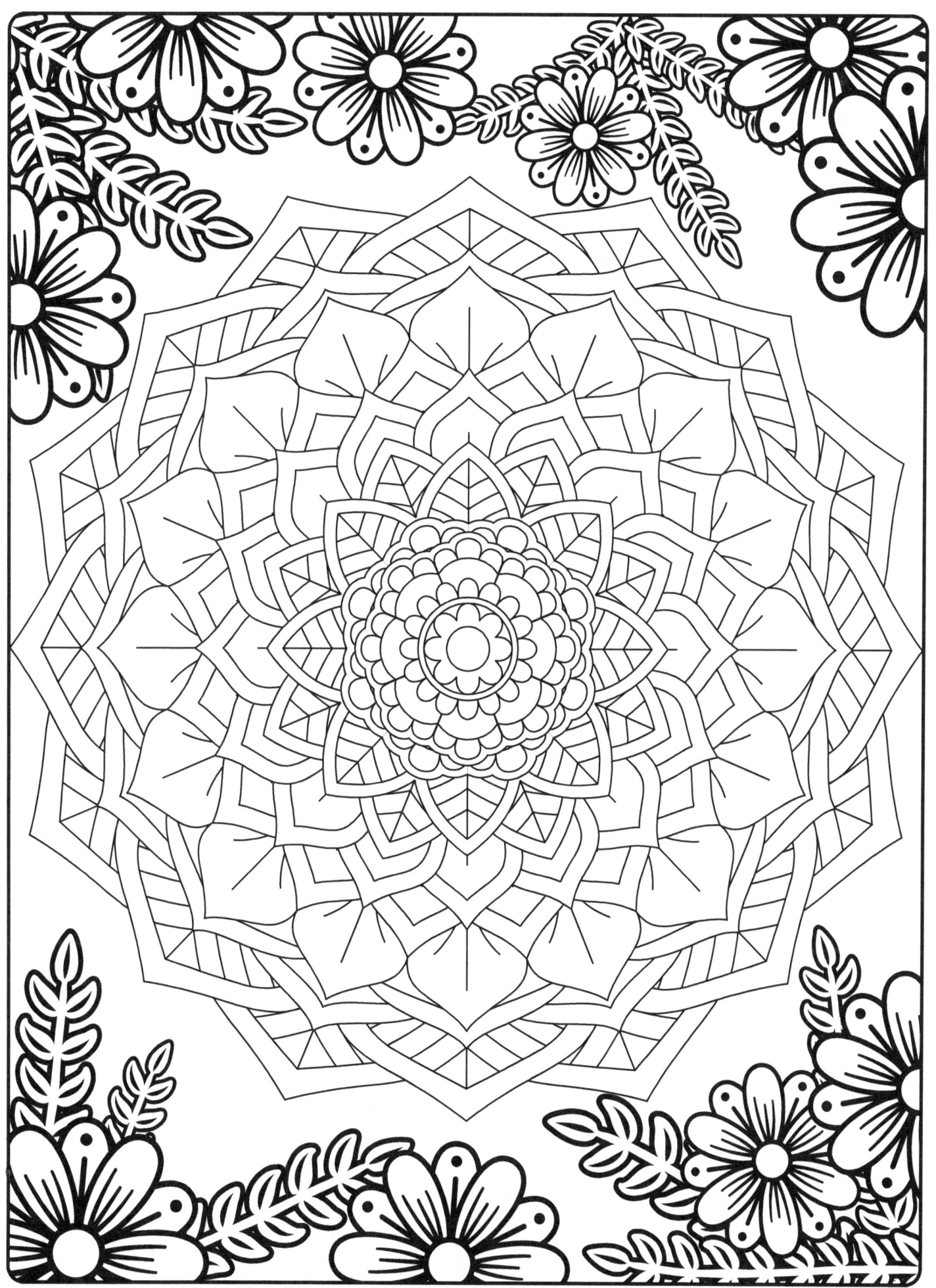

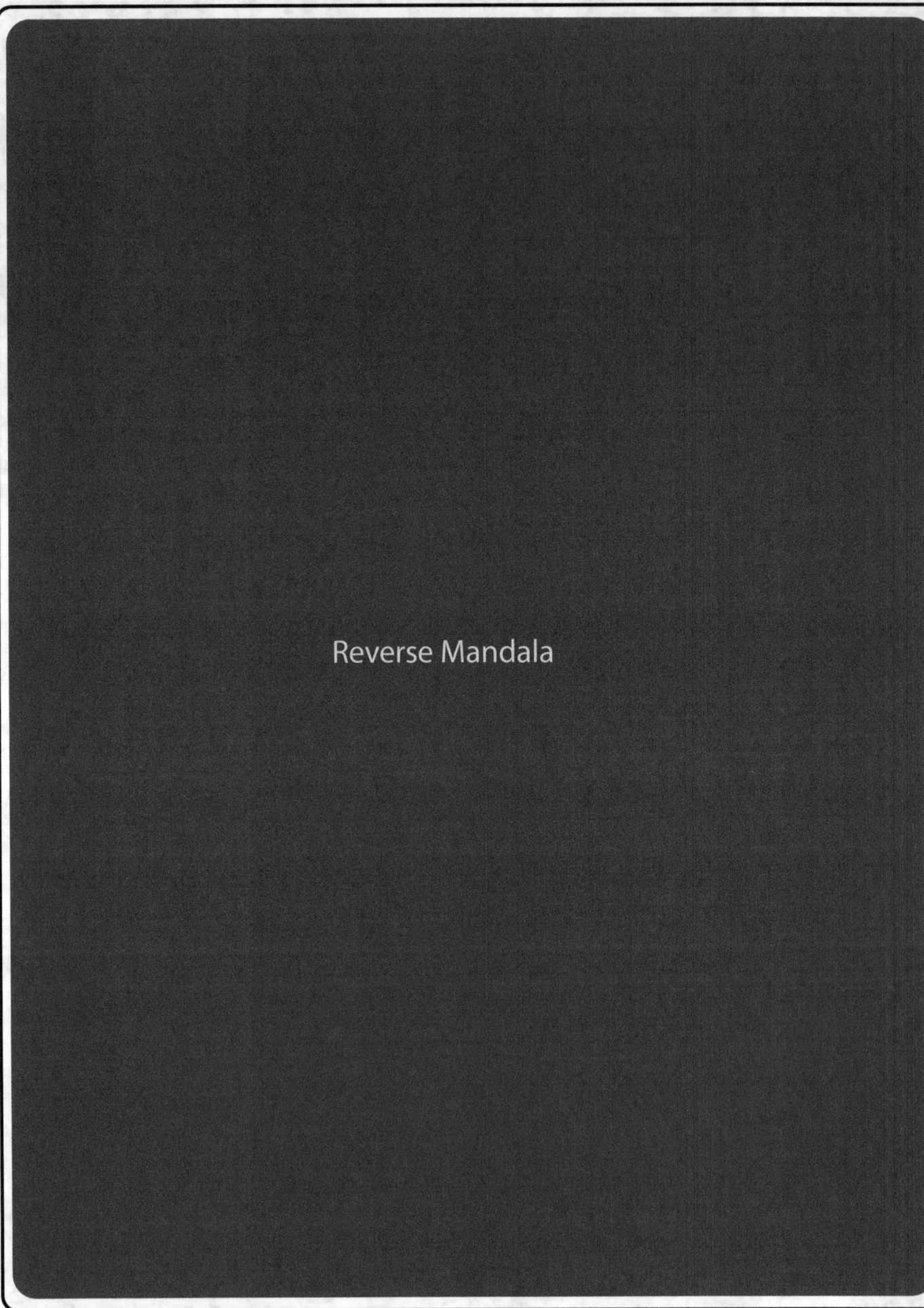

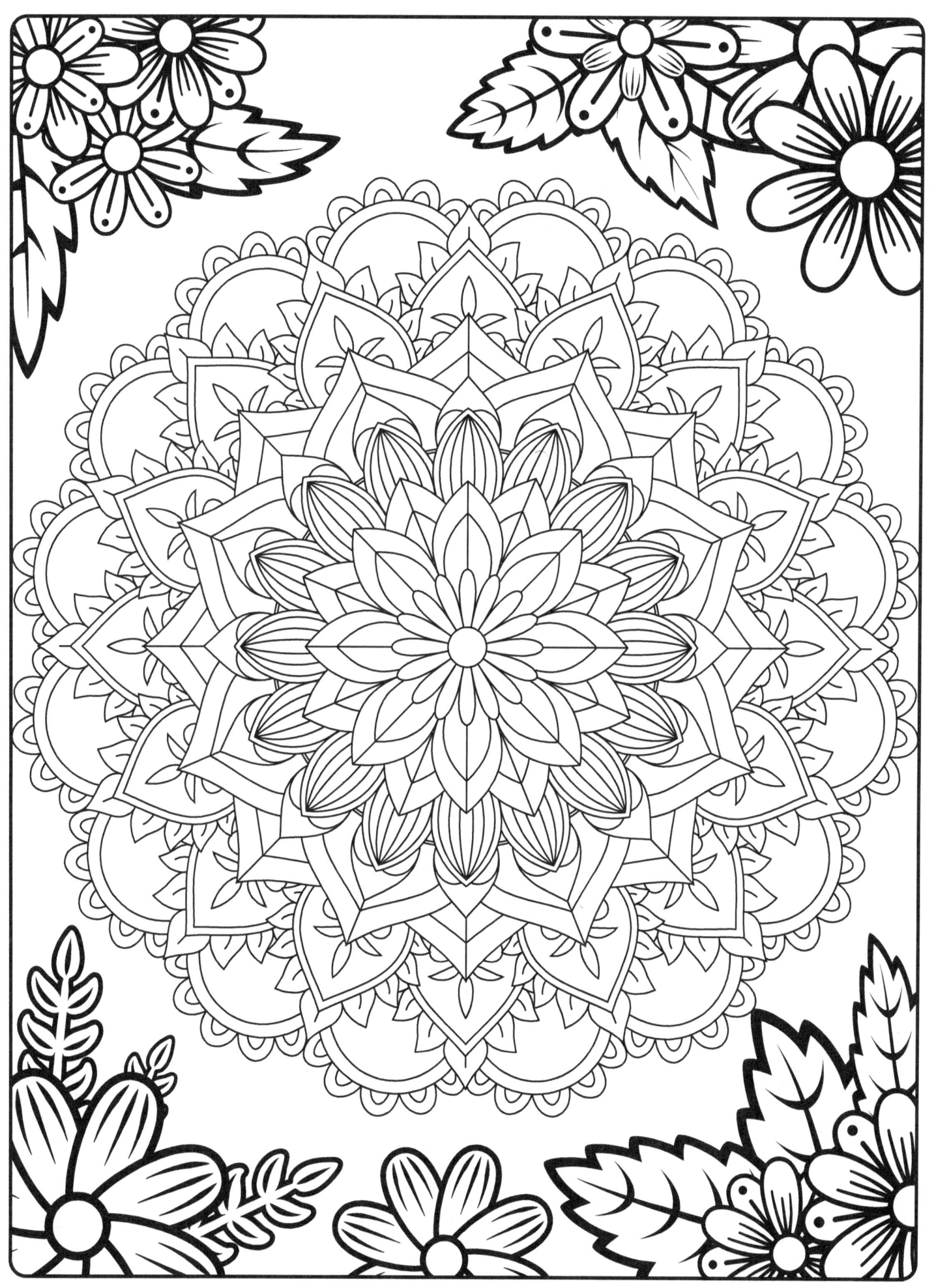

Reverse Mandala

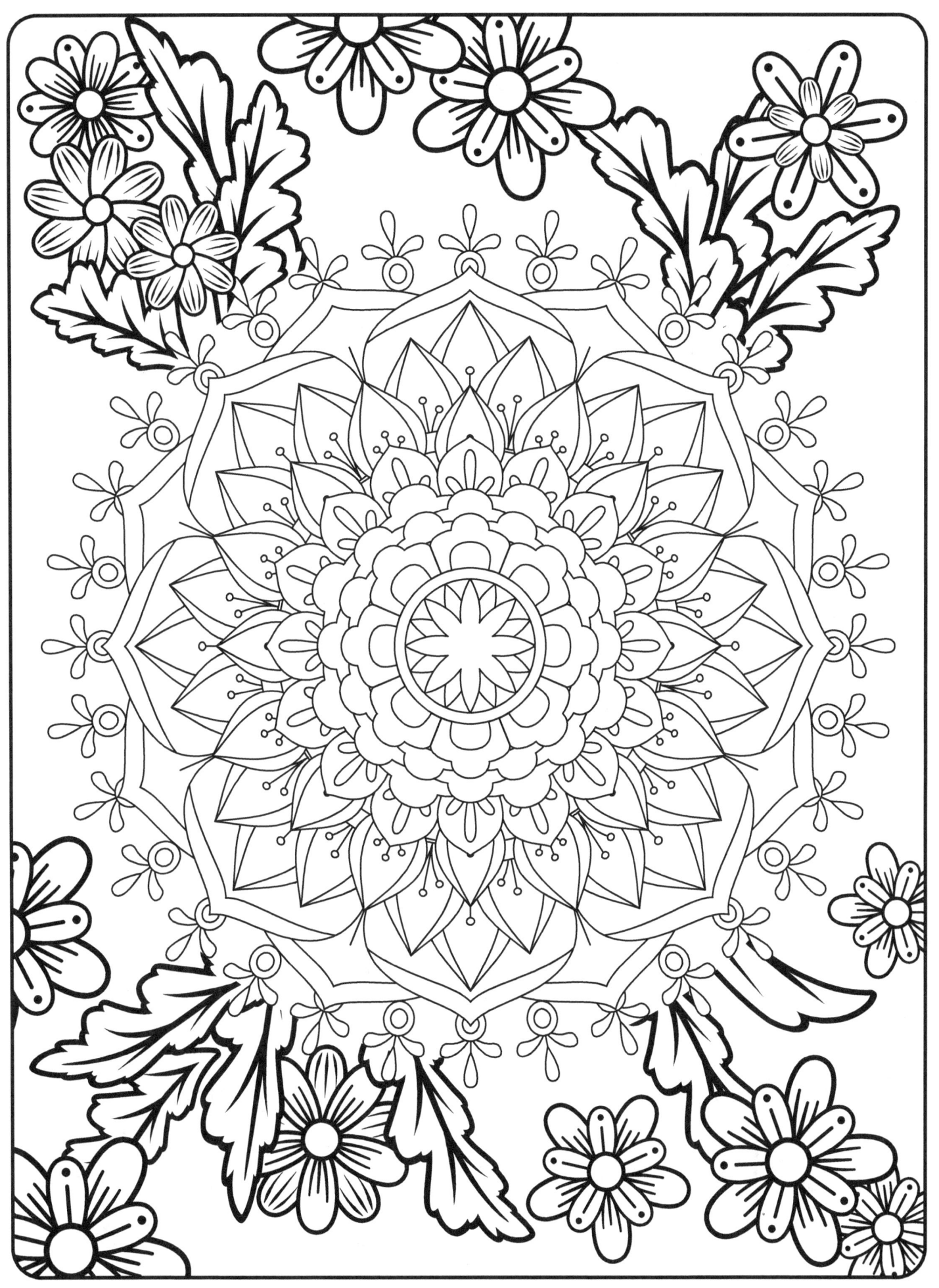

Reverse Mandala

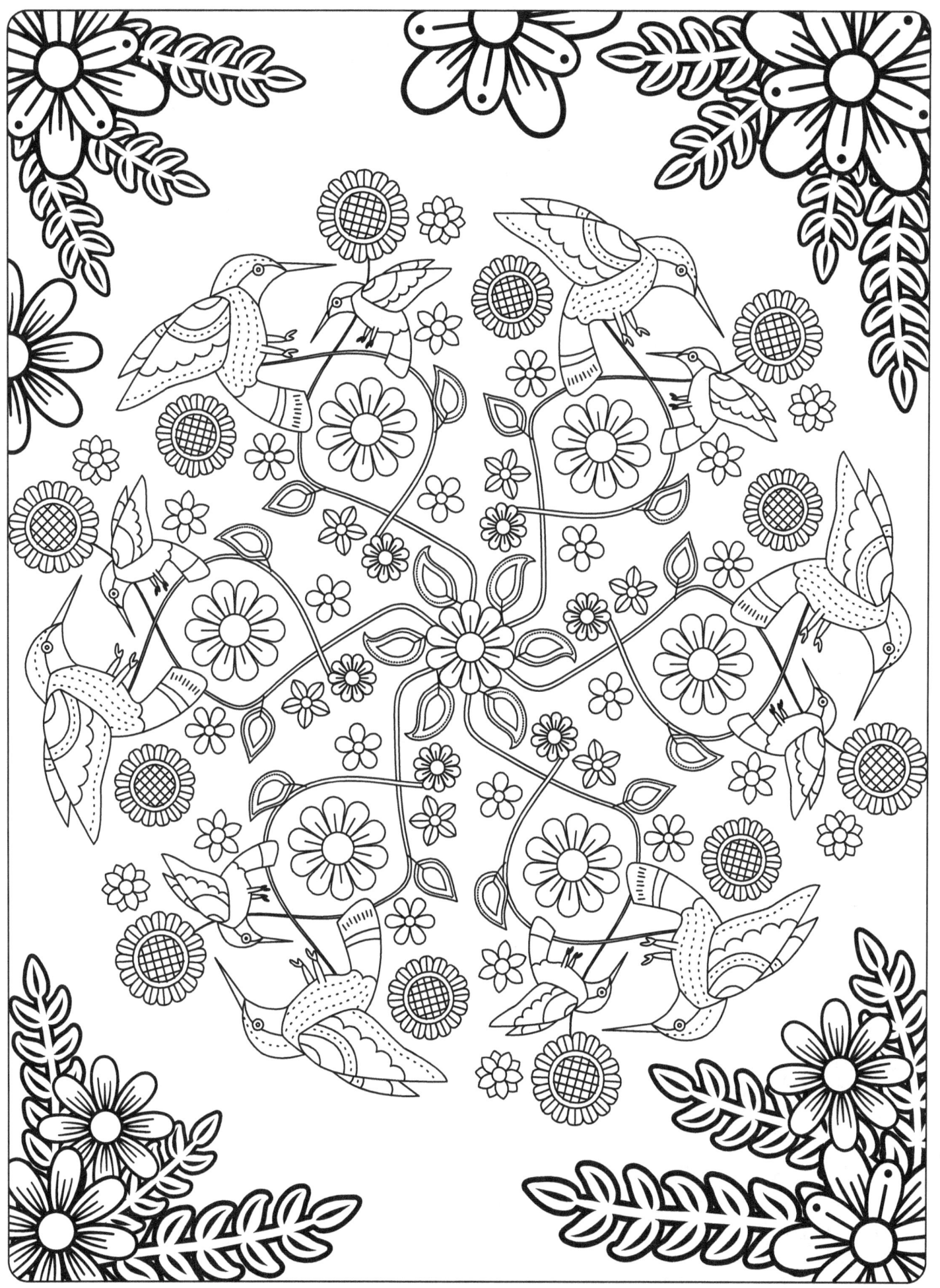

Reverse Mandala

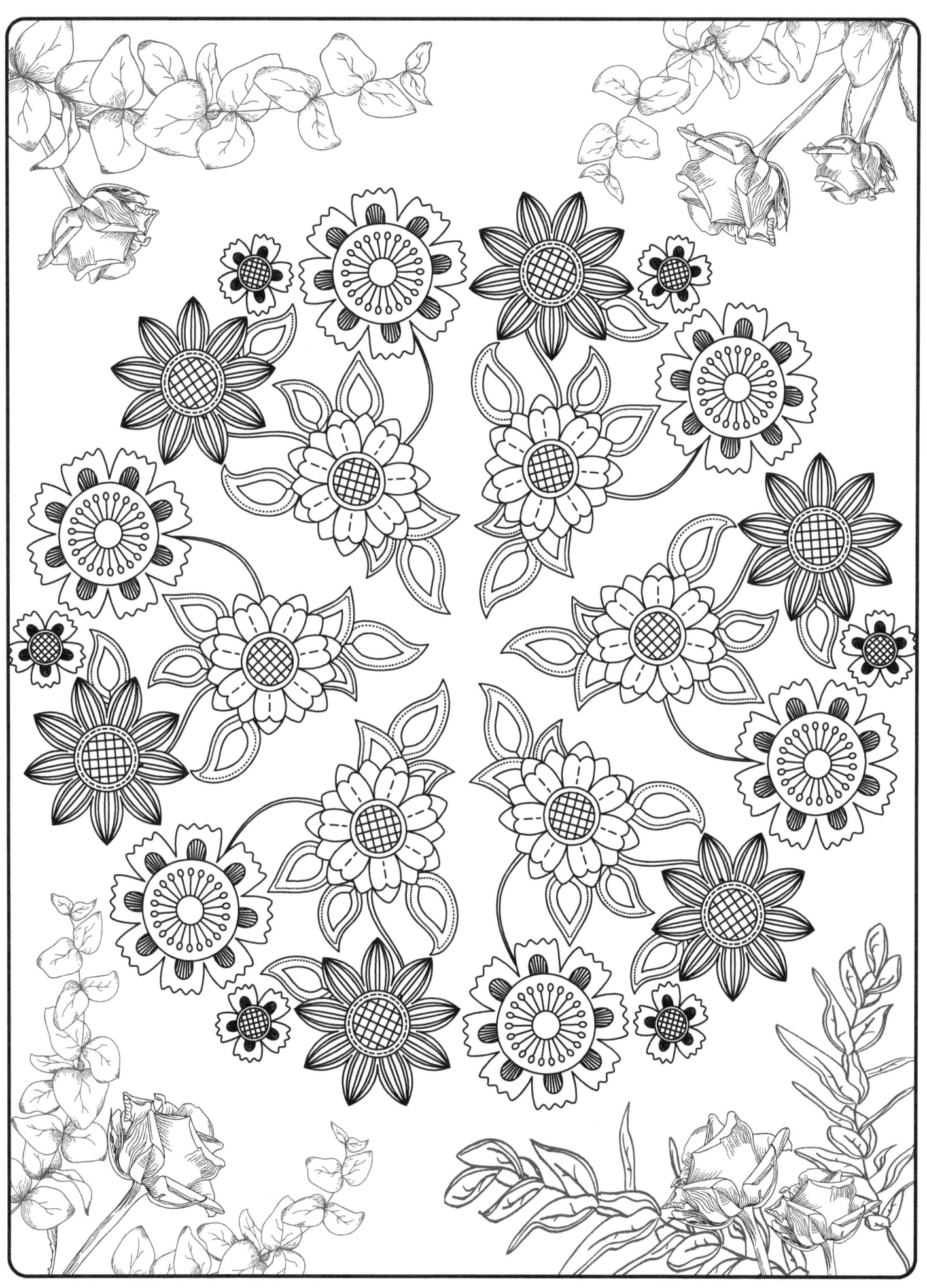

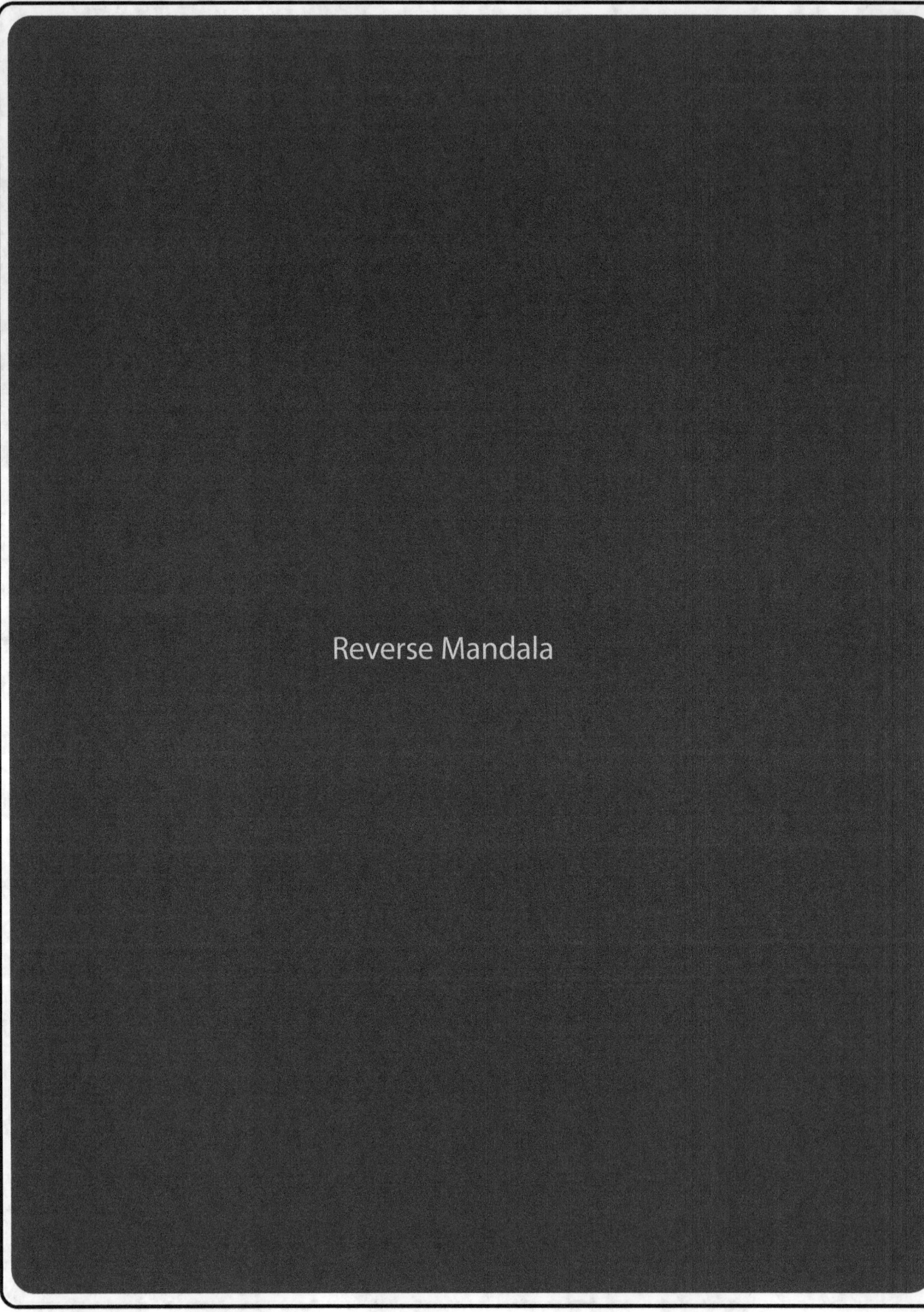

Reverse Mandala

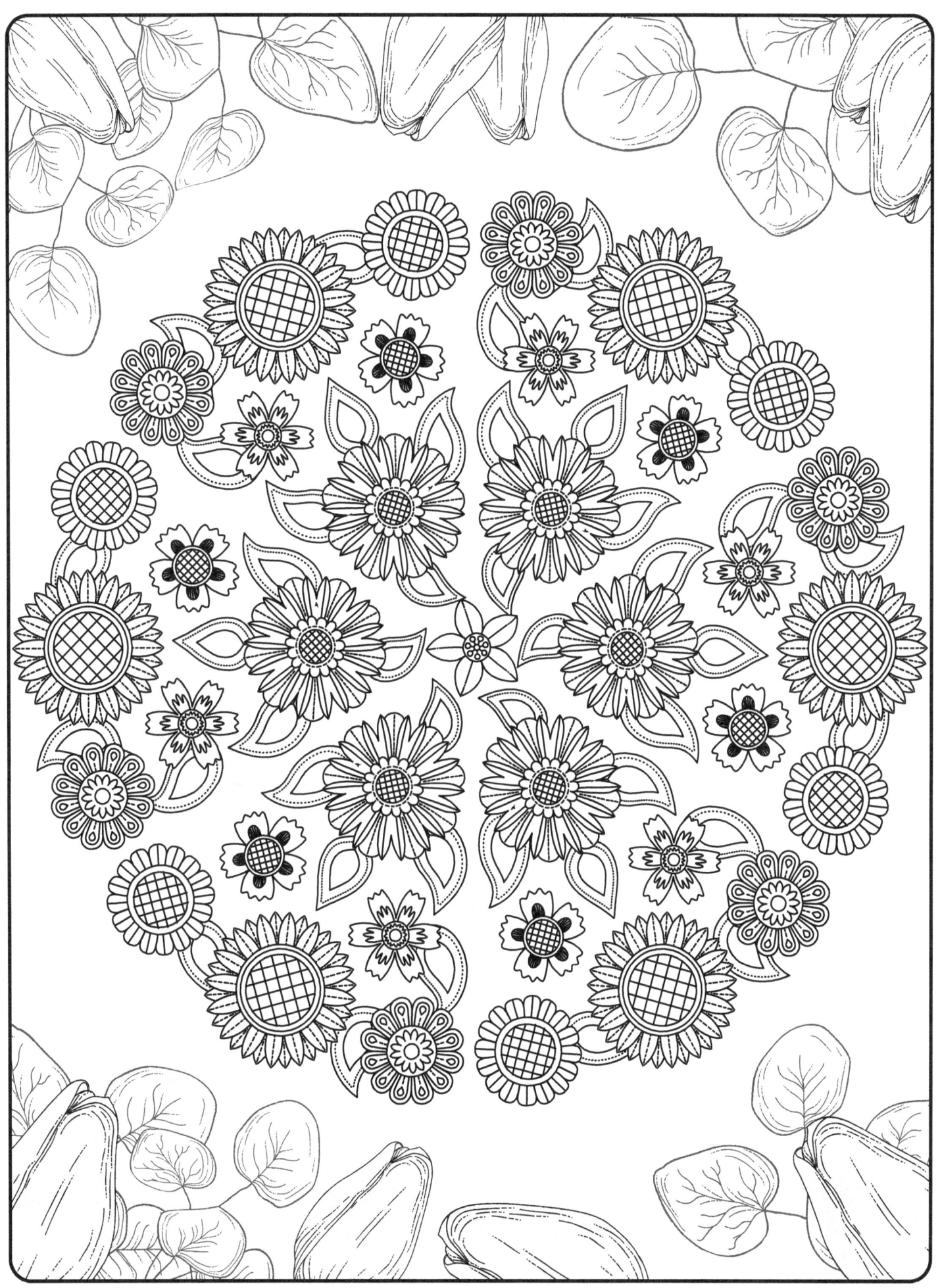

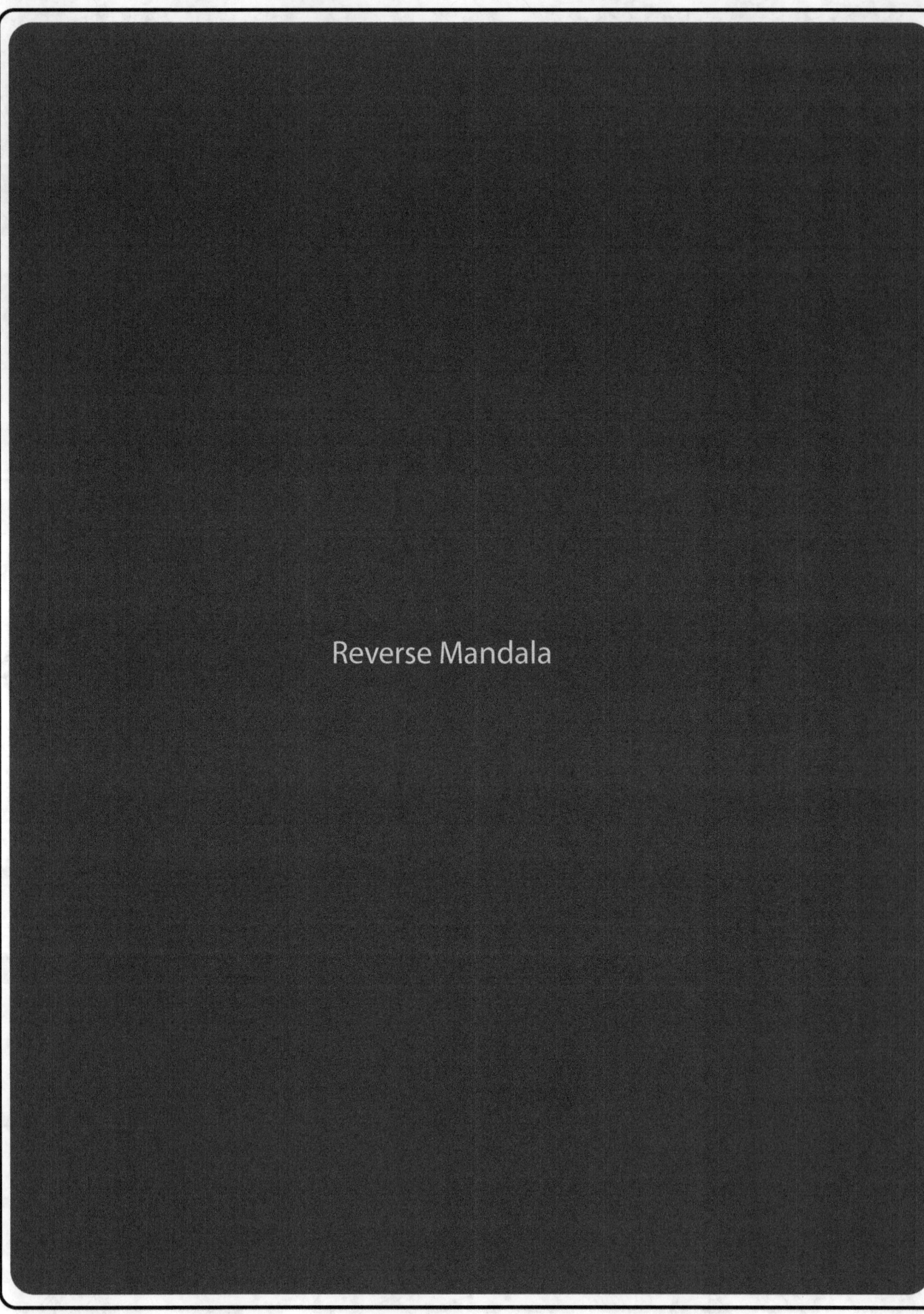

Reverse Mandala

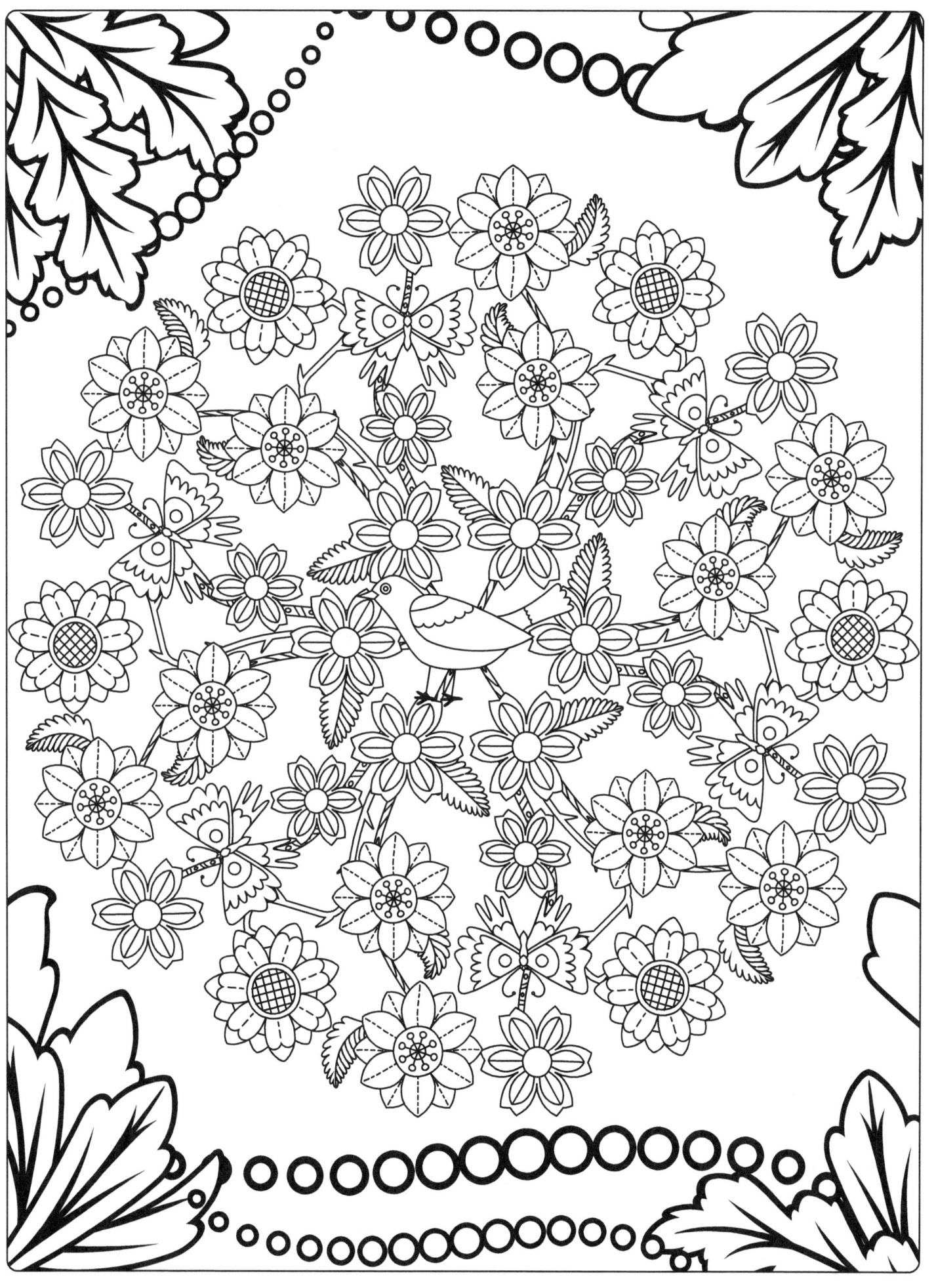

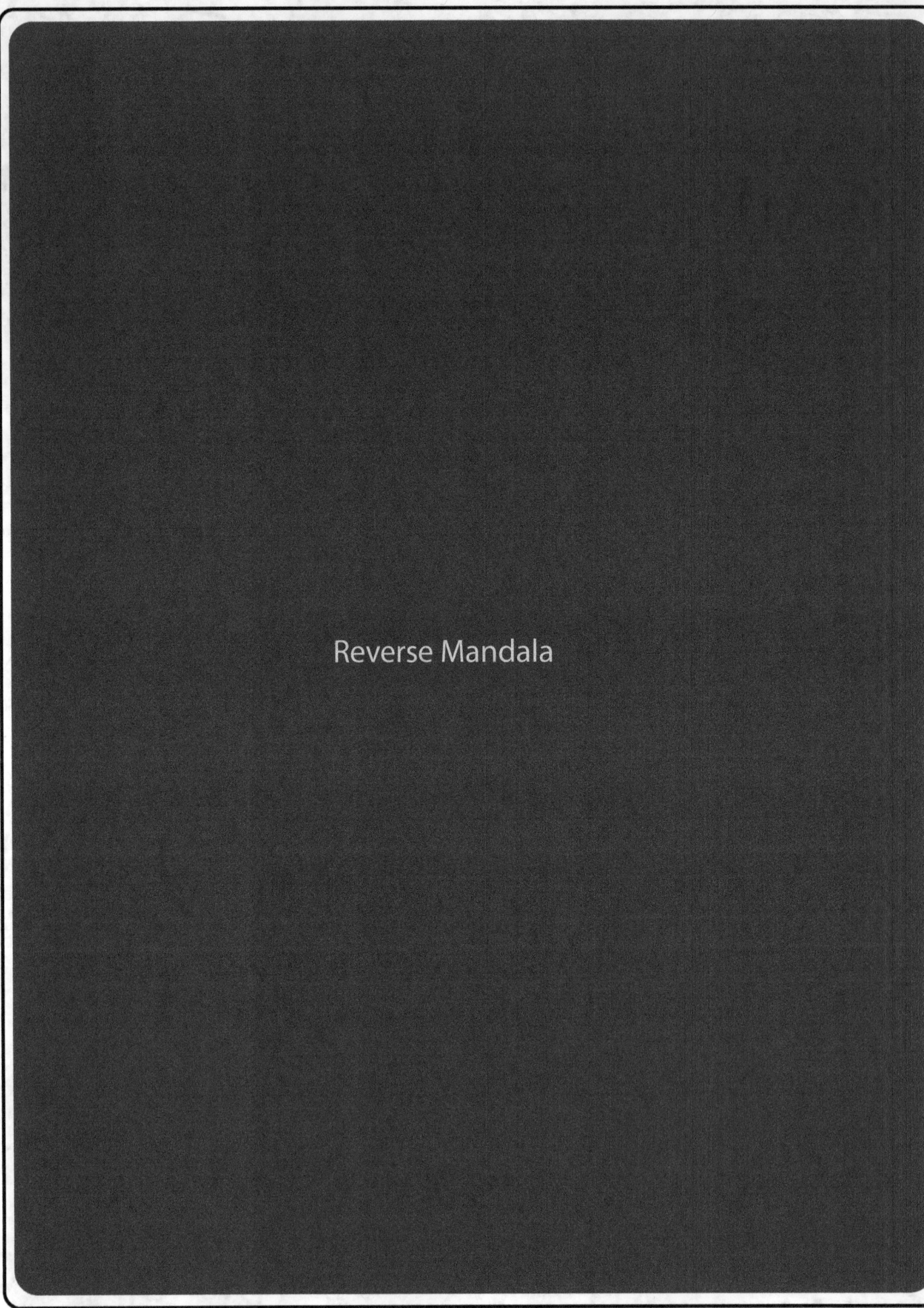

Reverse Mandala

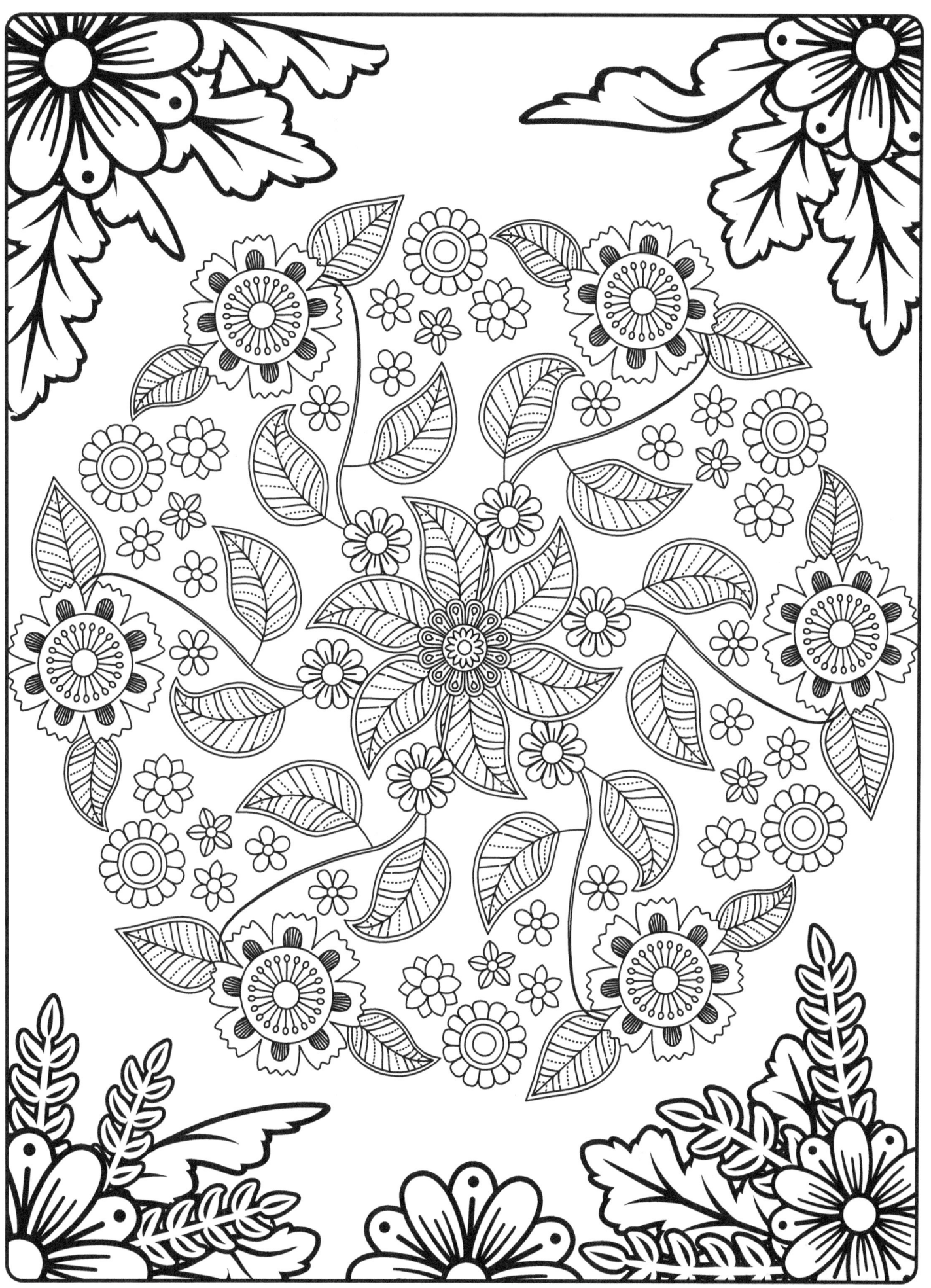

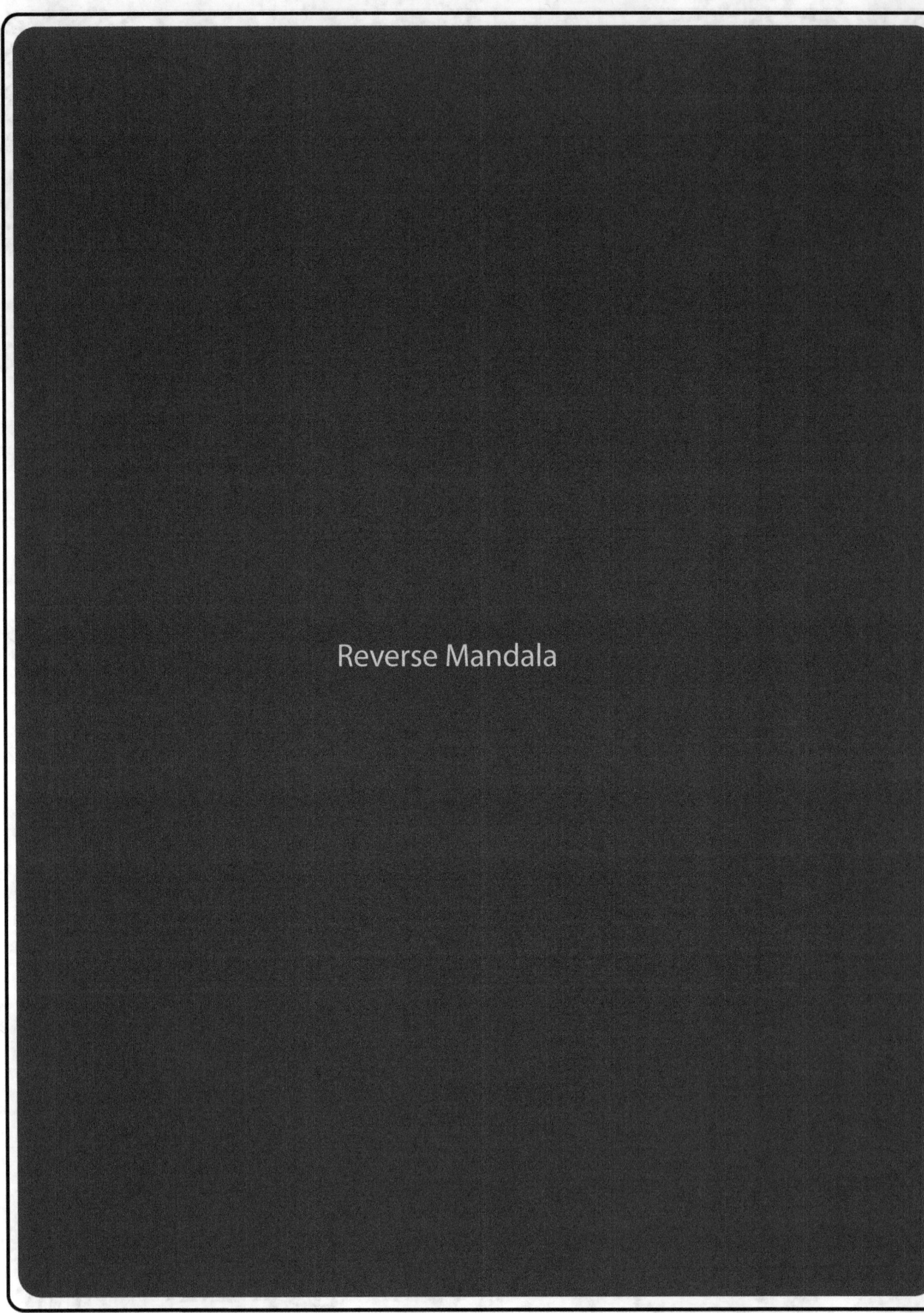
Reverse Mandala

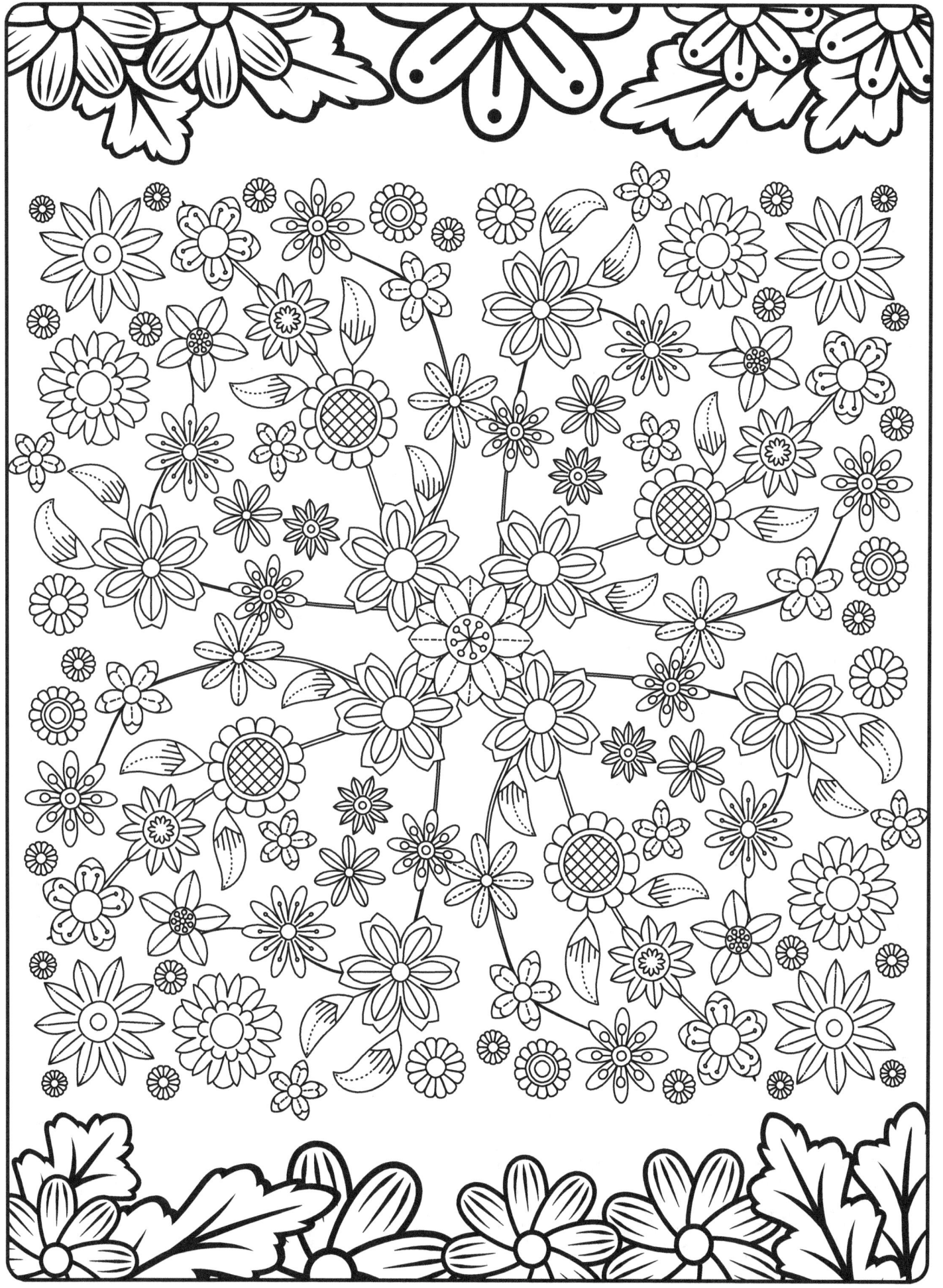

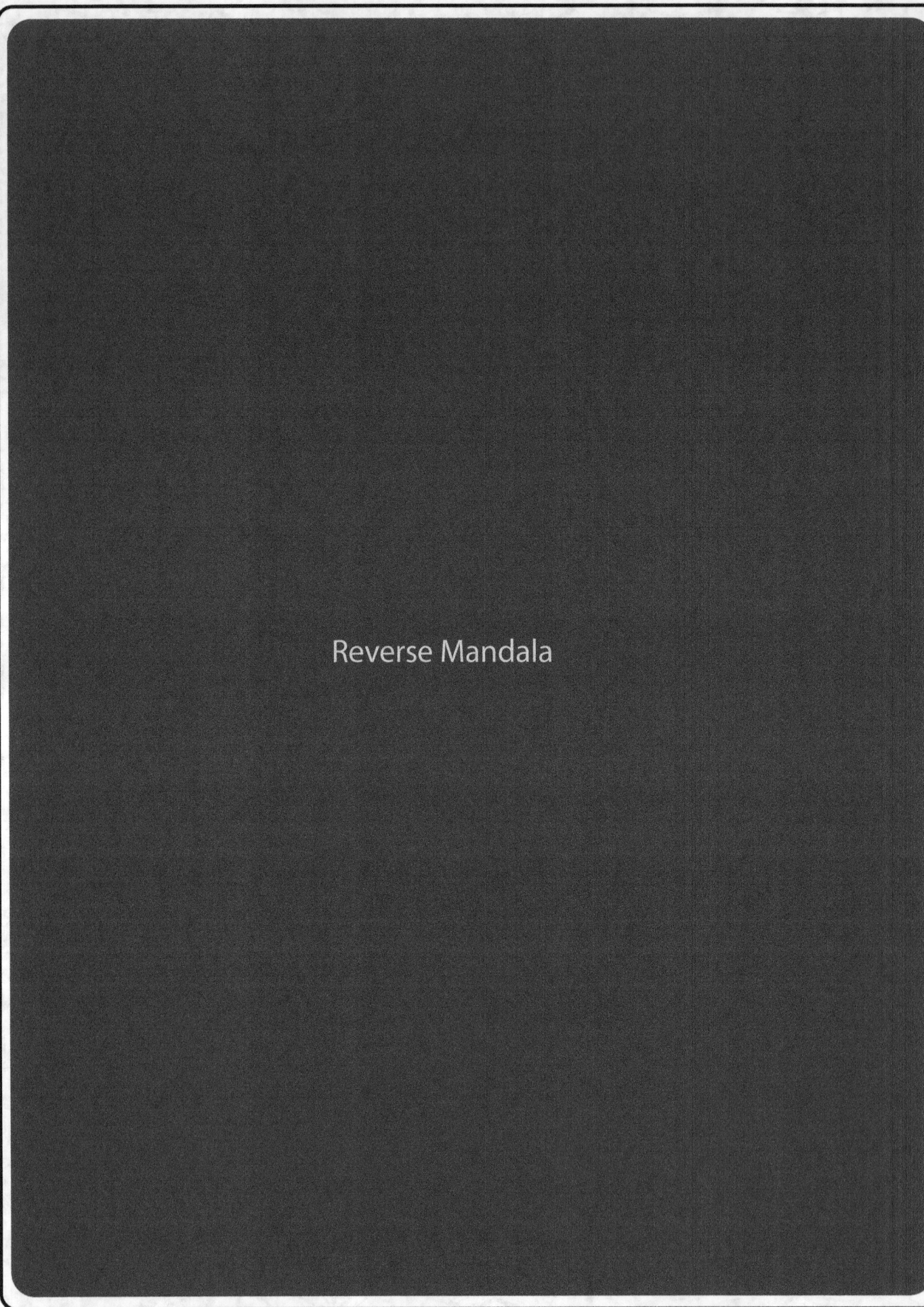

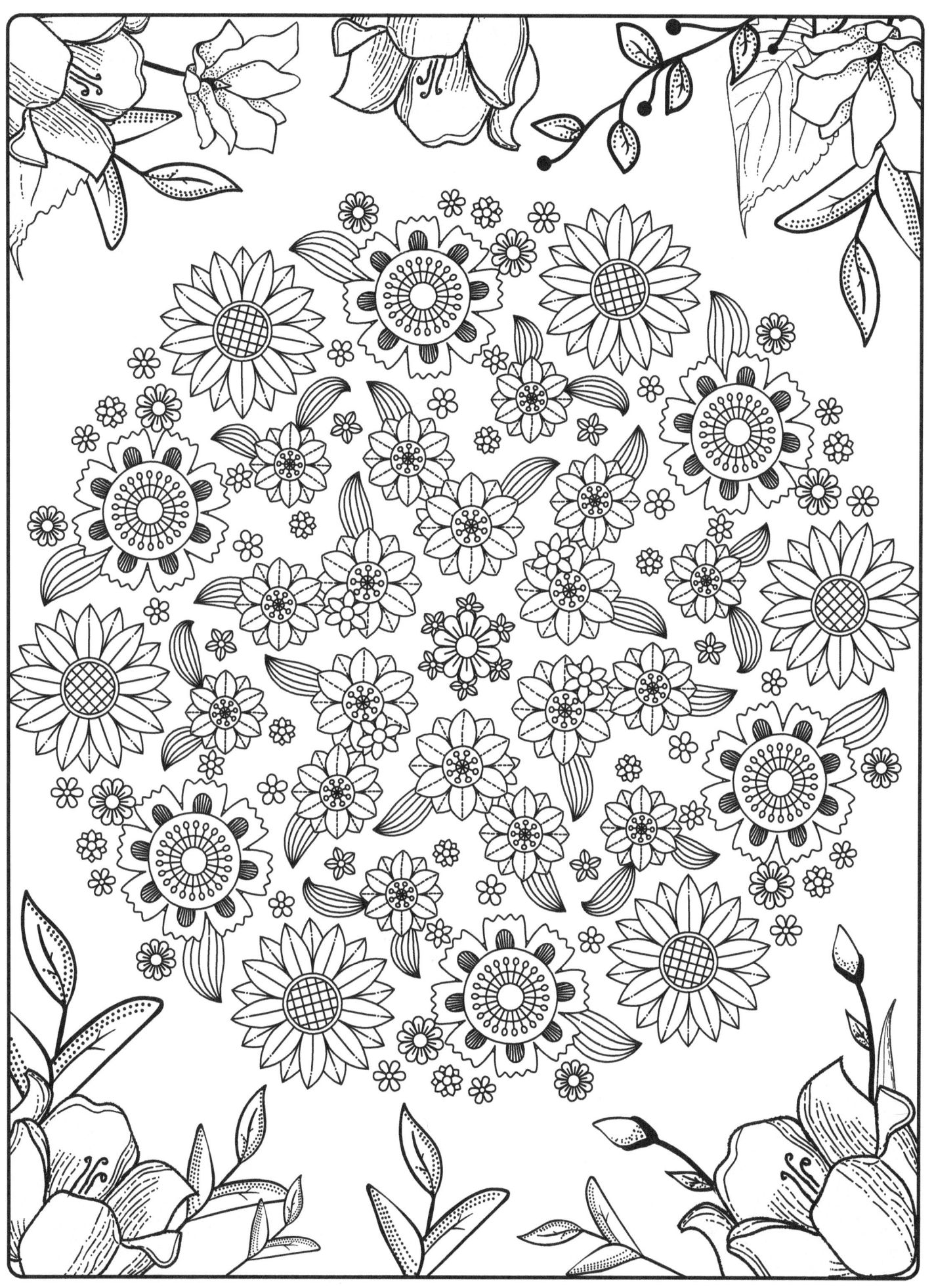

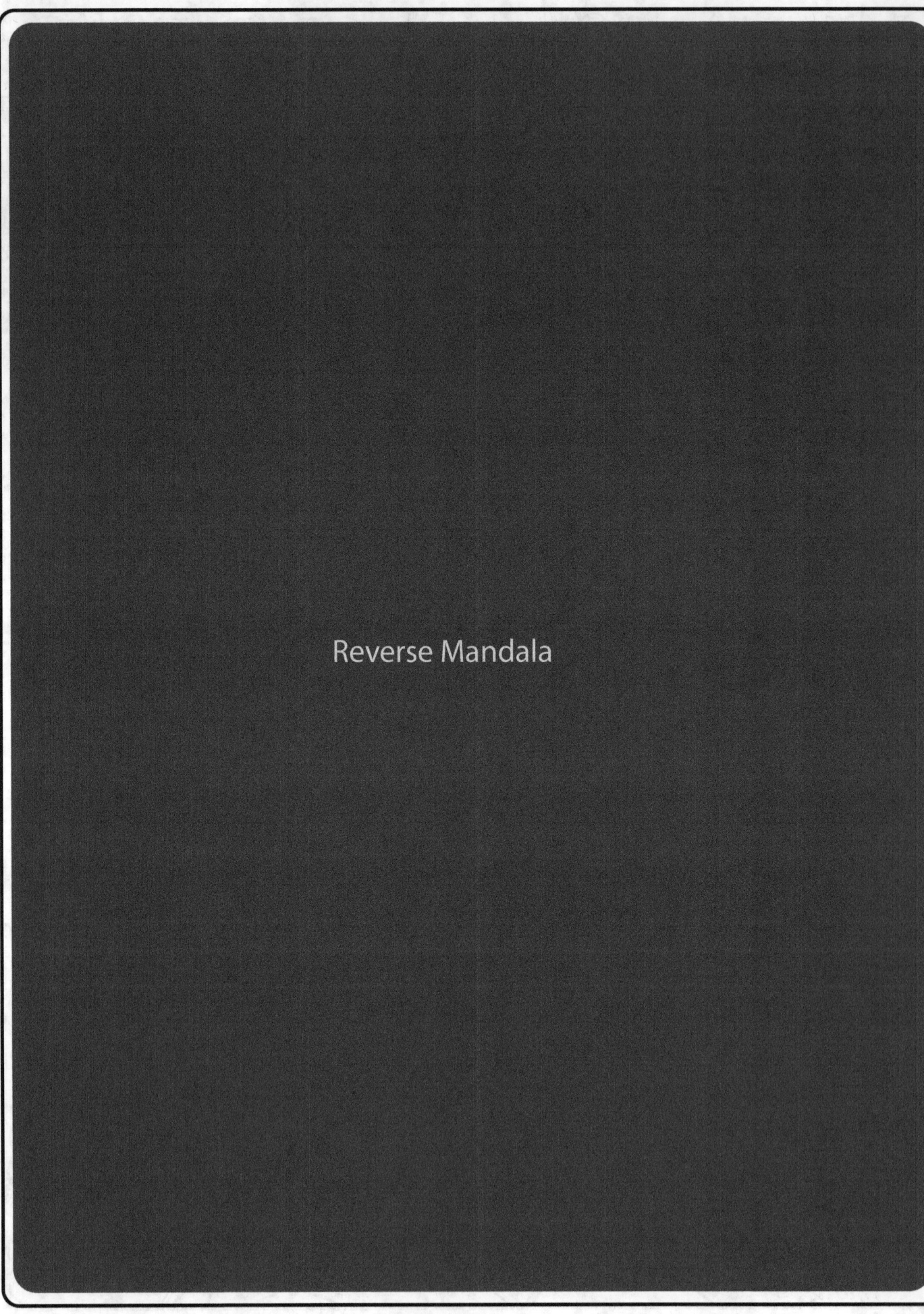

Reverse Mandala

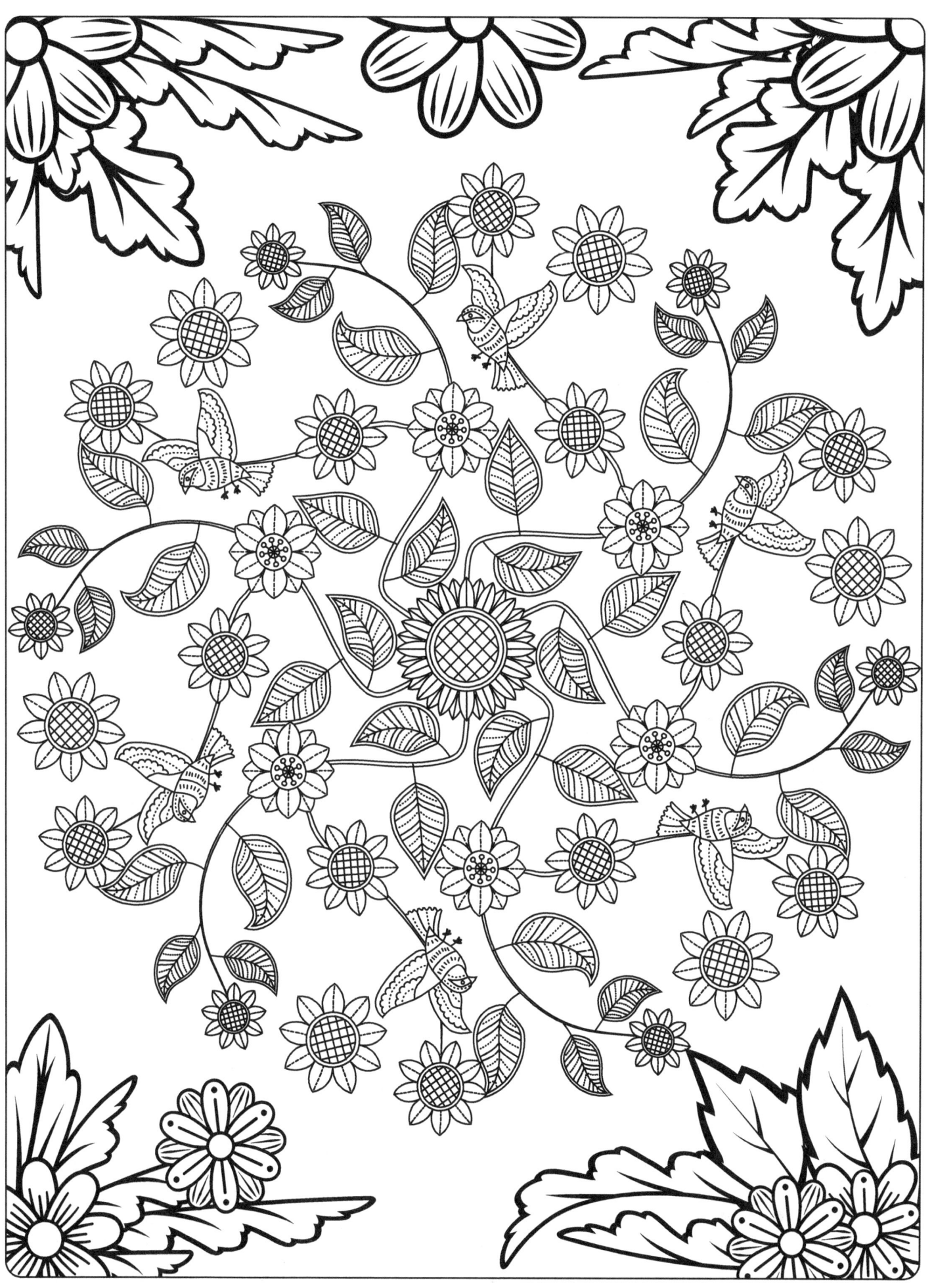

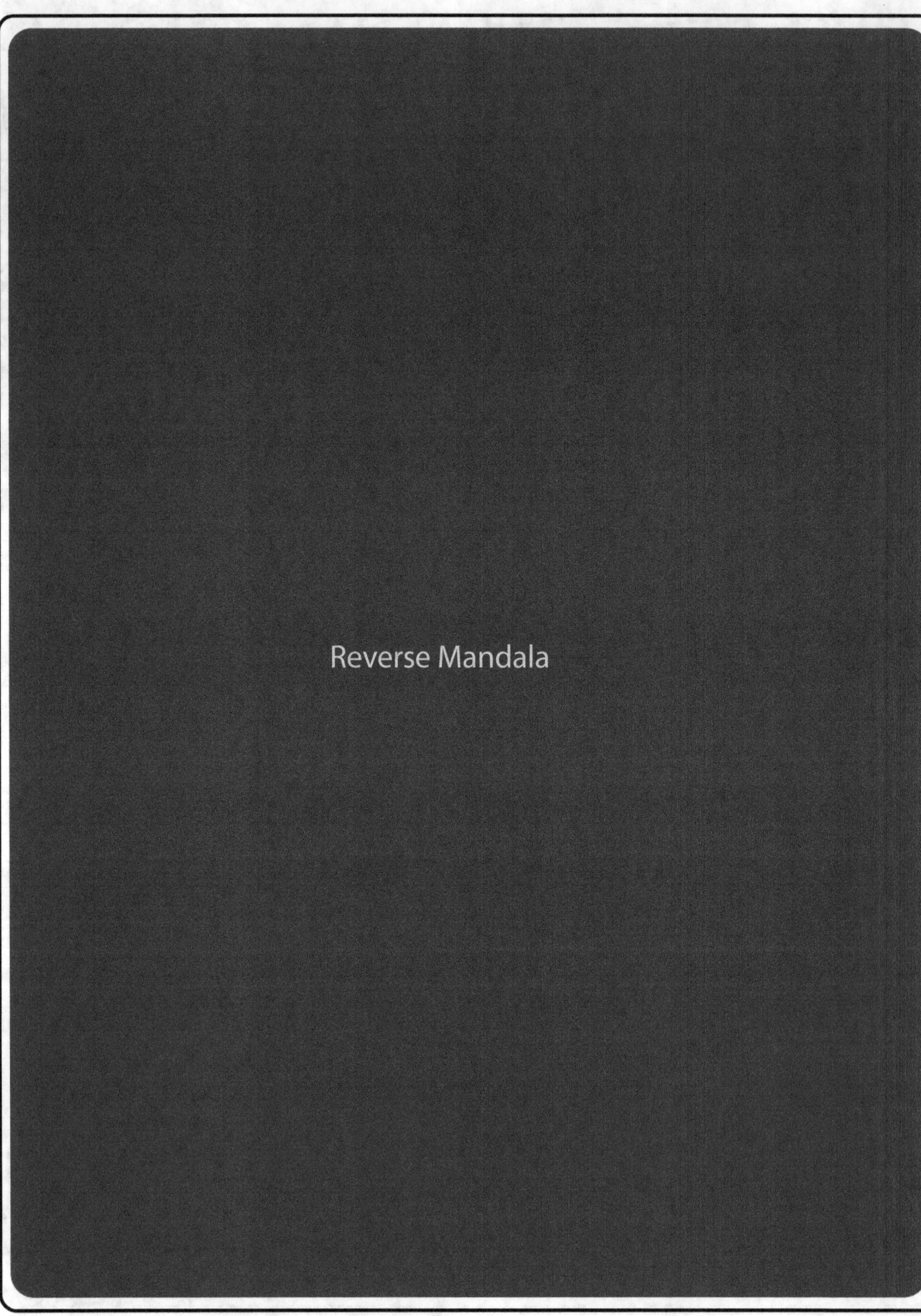
Reverse Mandala

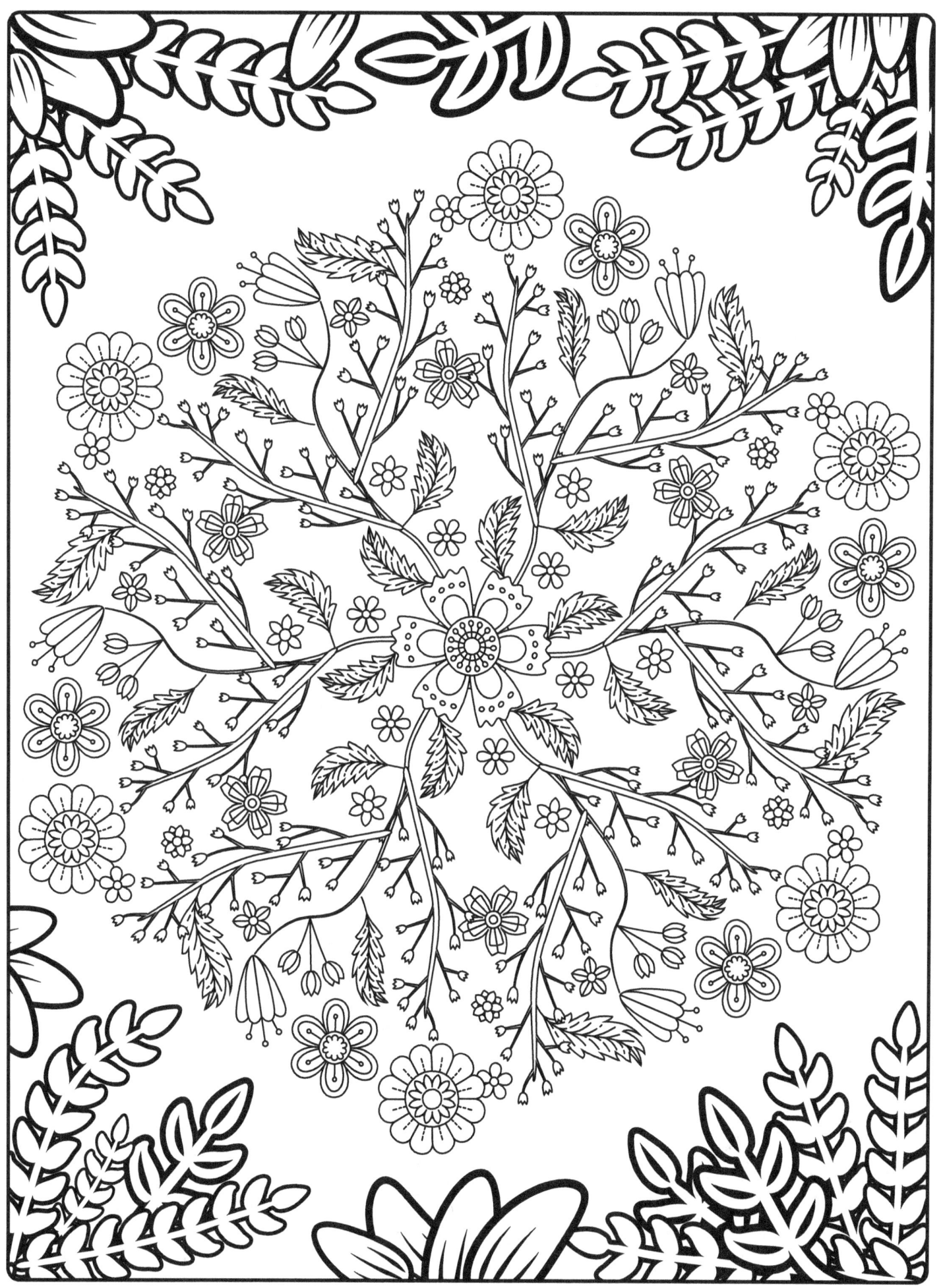

Reverse Mandala

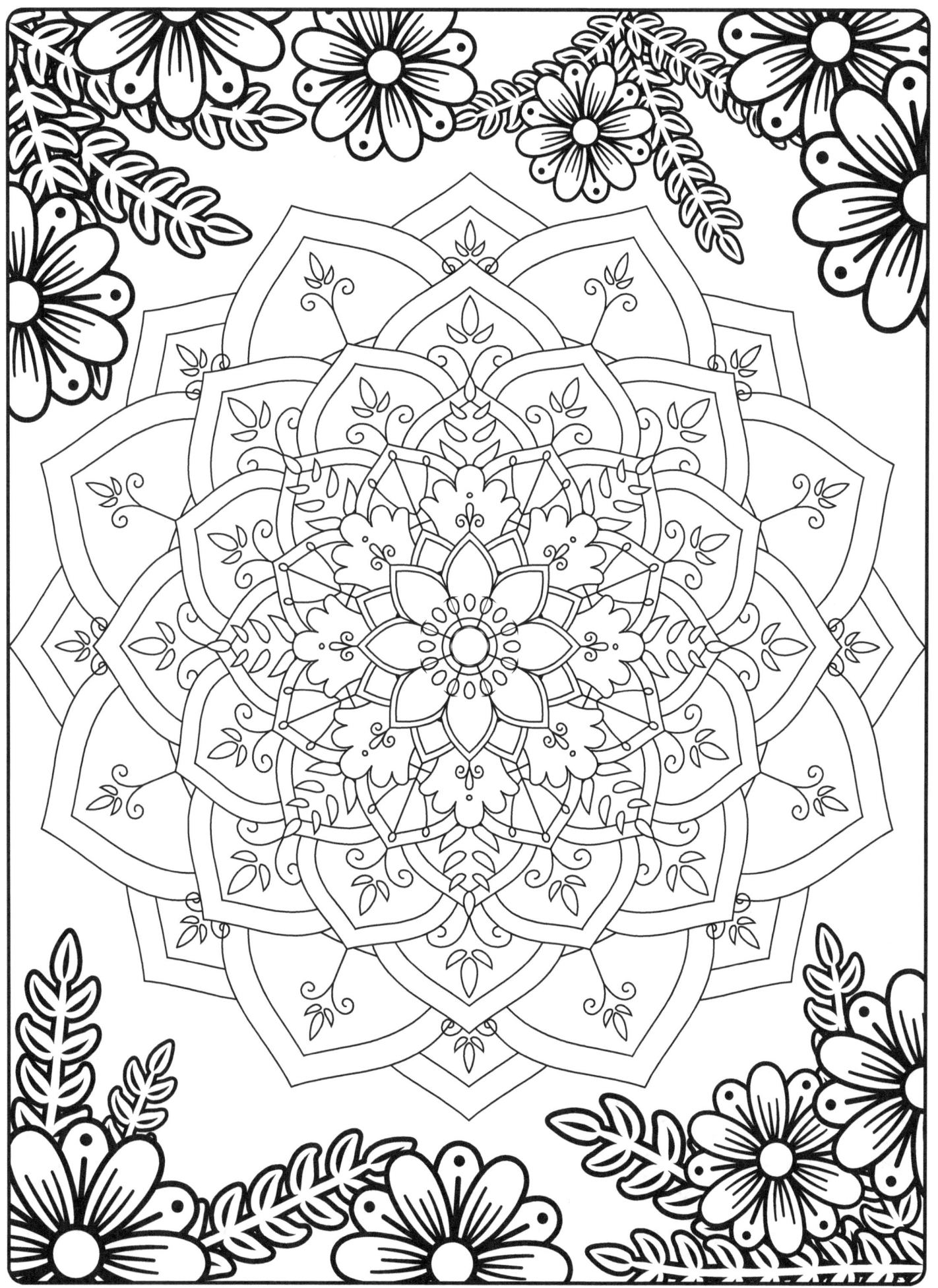

Reverse Mandala

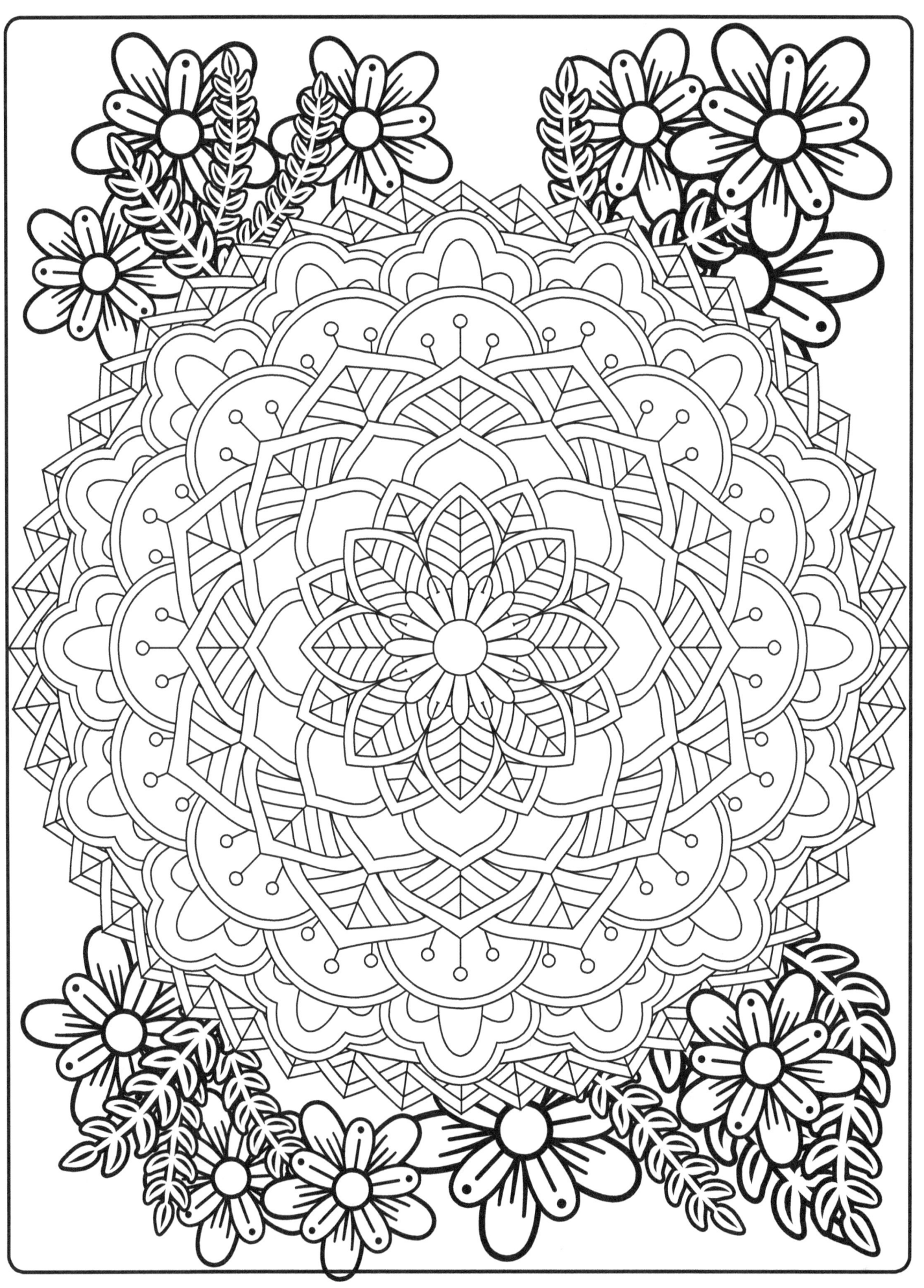

Reverse Mandala

www.ingramcontent.com/pod-product-compliance
Lightning Source LLC
Chambersburg PA
CBHW081441220526
45466CB00008B/2473